Coaching the
Spread Option Offense

Bobby Granger

D1157724

COACHES
CHOICE™

©2002 Coaches Choice. All rights reserved. Printed in the United States.

No part of this book may be reproduced, stored in a retrieval system, or transmitted, in any form or by any means, electronic, mechanical, photocopying, recording, or otherwise, without the prior permission of Coaches Choice.

ISBN: 1-58518-599-X
Library of Congress Control Number: 2001098605
Book layout: Jeanne Hamilton
Diagrams: Deborah Oldenburg
Cover design: Jennifer Bokelmann

Coaches Choice
P.O. Box 1828
Monterey, CA 93942
www.coacheschoice.com

DEDICATION

I would like to dedicate this book to my mother. She always had faith in me, even when she didn't agree with me. I would also like to dedicate this book to my children, Sierra, Crash, and Kozet.

ACKNOWLEDGMENTS

I would like to say how much I enjoyed working with all the different players and Texas high school coaches. I have made some tremendous friends and will always hold them close to my heart.

CONTENTS

Over the last 16 years in South Texas, I have had the pleasure of coaching football at nine different high schools, scouting for a tenth high school, and coaching receivers for a professional arena football team. I have implemented 10 different offensive systems while coaching every position along the way, and I've noted the positives and negatives of each. I have learned the fundamentals, practice organization, the strategy used, and most of all the type of personnel required for a successful football team.

Many of the schools I coached lacked the numbers, the athletes, the equipment, or they didn't have enough coaches and facilities. We had to find different ways to be successful. We did not have the athletes to just line up and beat our opponents, and I was always searching for better ways to be successful. In 1984, I read Tiger Ellison's book on the *run and shoot* and liked several of his ideas. A few years later I wrote to him about his book, then sent him my first playbook and asked him for his input.

We shared a few phone conversations and letters before he passed away. The one thing I will always remember was how he believed in his offense. He believed in the mix of the option with the pass. I wanted to take this concept and combine it with the Veer, a pro-passing attack that uses picks, balanced formations, and a flexible audible system. The result is the spread option offense.

THE FOUR KEYS

In 1988, I wrote an article that was published in *Texas Coach* called the "Four Keys." It was a short article on what I believed were the factors of being a successful coach. These four keys were teaching proper fundamentals, organizing practice, using strategy during games, and recognizing talent. When I decided to write this book, I wanted to keep in mind the principles of these four keys.

Teaching Proper Fundamentals

The first key to being a successful coach is to know the proper fundamentals of each position and how to teach them. In football, coaches tend to forget the importance of fundamentals. For example, coaches find execution breakdowns because of improper first steps and aiming points. At all levels, coaches must teach the proper fundamentals on a daily basis, or the team's level of play will suffer.

Motivation, both positive and negative, is a part of teaching, and coaches have successfully used both types of motivation. But the bottom line is teaching the correct fundamentals *on the go*. On the go means the players are executing the fundamentals through individual, half lines, inside/outside hulls (groups), 7-on-7, and team drills. Some coaches just talk too much, instead of really working their players' skills.

Organizing Practice

After coaches have learned the proper fundamentals and know how to teach them, organizing practice becomes an important second key. You have only so many minutes in the day, so in order to get ahead of your opponents, plan to accomplish more than they do in the same amount of time. Practicing proper repetition is the name of the game. The practice schedule of individual, group, and team segments should correlate with the personnel used in the game. Many times during games coaches get a brainstorm and substitute players with better talent for a particular play. What usually happens is the play is a bust because of a lack of execution.

Coaches should type or write out the entire practice schedule. Break down every phase (individual, group, and team) into five-minute periods. Name each drill and all the plays in the group and team segments. In the team phase, script plays so that you practice what you plan to use in the games. Do not spend a quarter of the time on one specific play that you use only once or twice in a game. Scripting helps coaches to observe their positions better because they know in advance what the play will be.

Organization also applies to how you use your other coaches. To get the most out of each person and benefit the program, evaluate the ability of each coach and give him specific responsibilities. During practices and games, the position coach or coordinator should be the only person correcting or teaching his players. When a player has two or three different coaches teaching him, it is more difficult for him to concentrate. If another coach sees a fundamental or technique that can be improved, he should go to that position coach and make the suggestion. This allows the position coach to weigh the information and decide what he feels is important without losing respect from his players or fellow coaches.

You have several options when dividing practice into individual, group, and team sections. One factor to consider has to be the numbers and whether you team two platoons. Some successful teams go almost straight team and hammer the Junior Varsity team with two groups. Other teams just go half lines in group because of low numbers. Regardless, the constant variable for success is coaching *on the go*.

Using Strategy During Games

The third key is strategy. But before talking about strategy, it should be emphasized that it doesn't matter what strategy you use if the offensive line can't sustain a double-team or a stalemate block. Too many times coaches get excited about schemes and forget about personnel. Don't throw in the towel because you don't have the personnel up front to base block, but take it into account when you evaluate what will be successful.

The best offensive strategy is to control the clock and score every possession. But game strategy is related to your personnel, knowledge, opponent's ability, wind and weather conditions, field position, score, and time in the game. Also, consider what plays you have run in practice. Never call a play that you did not practice during the week. Do not expect players to fully execute any type of play that you did not cover in detail in practice the week before.

Because turnovers usually determine why teams lose games, they always have to be considered when calling plays. Many times turnovers relate to teaching fundamentals. For example, if you allow the quarterback to throw into crowds, or try to ride the fullback on the inside veer, turnovers can occur. You have many successful offenses to choose from, and only you can decide which one is best for your team. The spread option offense is a great choice because it is versatile, puts pressure on defenses, and is based on finesse.

Recognizing Talent

The fourth key, recognition of talent, is by far the most important. When your team's talent is superior to your opponent's, it makes up for poor teaching, lack of organization, and poor strategy. That doesn't mean your team is going to win, but it gives them a better chance to win.

You should learn exactly what each player's strengths are and how to use these qualities to help your team. You have to know where to play the best athletes, but also where to hide the poor athletes. When a program has low numbers, the job of picking the best players is easier. When a program has a large number of good players, the task of selecting players for each position becomes more difficult. As you go up in a higher classification of football, recognition and differentiation of talent becomes more difficult.

FINESSE OFFENSE

Controlling the ball and scoring is the goal of any offense. But scoring is more important than possession time. Winning depends on scoring without turning the ball over, then relying on the defense and special teams. When you coach at schools that lack athletes and numbers, you need to search for ways to be successful without them.

The inside veer is a good choice as the base running play for the spread option offense for these four reasons:

1. It allows the offensive line to double-team at the point of attack.

2. It neutralizes the defensive end without blocking him.

3. It confuses the responsibilities of linebackers and safeties.

4. It works with four wide receivers in a run/pass audible scheme.

Spread refers to the passing attack. The majority of the route combinations use some type of pick. You should teach how to pick defenders without having offensive pass interference called. Most of these routes are progression or position reads. Most of the routes are a pick or a rub for these four reasons:

1. It lets you predetermine a receiver on the progression read.

2. It allows lesser athletes to get open.

3. Picks can work short or deep.

4. Picks in five-step drop backs help prevent sacks.

Balanced Formations and Audibles

Balanced formations and audibles are two important concepts of this finesse offense. They are used to attack certain defensive personnel and weaknesses in their alignment. By combining the balanced formations with different types of motions, you force the defense to also align balanced or to expose the weak flank. That is why audibles are so important. Audibles keep the offense out of bad plays and allow it to take advantage of personnel mismatches and alignments.

Today, many defenses use specific types of personnel on the strongside and weakside of their defense. Offensively, you should exploit positions that are not accustomed to certain types of plays. For example, make the free safety, not the strong safety, take on the toss. Also, run directly at weakside linebackers with isolation plays and make bigger and slower linebackers attempt to cover receivers on passes.

Many coaches hesitate to use audibles because of the power they give the quarterback. But if you do a great job in selecting the quarterback, and then teach him when and how to make good decisions, your quarterback will use that power well.

Defense Comes First

Defense first is another consideration in using this offense. A strong defense is essential to your team. If you team two platoons, stronger athletes should be placed on defense. Even when teams have several players going both ways, they should never come off the field on defense. If players are going to rest, it should always be when the offense has the ball. The spread option offense does not rely on great linemen or fast receivers to be successful.

With the inside veer, 175-pound offensive guards and tackles can double-team the 240-pound defensive tackle. Besides double-team blocks, allowing a player to run himself out of a play is also effective.

Pass blocking does not require offensive linemen to drive defenders. As long as the offensive linemen can keep defensive linemen out of the pocket for two or three seconds, the receivers can pick for each other. Even though you want big strong tight ends, the spread option offense does not require them. Instead, those big strong tight-end types can play defensive end and linebacker.

Personnel Needed

For this offense to be successful, you need an intelligent quarterback who can move and throw an accurate pass. For the option, he doesn't have to be fast, but must have the composure to read and stay on the line of scrimmage. Pressure cannot affect this individual. For the spread, he can be either short or tall as long as he can throw a football 40 yards accurately. He must also be able to concentrate on staying in the pocket and throwing the ball. For audibles, he must have the ability to follow directions and execute them during the game. (Chapter 15 examines the qualities needed for each offensive position in greater detail.)

The fullback needs to be strong and quick off the snap. He must be able to hold on to the football and block. He doesn't have to be a great runner, but he must be tough. If you do not have someone that fits this description, you should look at your quicker guards to fill this position.

The split and tight ends do not have to be fast or tall, but it does help. The ends must be able to catch the ball in the open and the middle. A coach should give up speed before pass catching ability. Because the ends align tight and split, a coach can fill the formations by substituting.

The backs are the fastest offensive players. They should be able to get the ball to the corner, run up between the tackles, and catch a pass. They must also be in great condition because of the motions used in the offense.

The linemen must be able to move their feet. They have to be smart enough to remember the plays and execute the audibles. But most of all, they have to want contact and get under pads.

CHAPTER 1

Spread Option Scheme

THE INSIDE VEER AND PICKS

Every team usually hangs their hat on a specific play. The inside veer is the base-running play in the spread option offense. This forces opponents to prepare for the true triple option. The quarterback reads the first defender over the playside tackle for his give/keep decision. If he doesn't give the ball, he attacks downhill and decides whether to keep it or pitch it to the motion back (Figure 1-1).

The playside tackle blocks hard inside and releases any defender head-up or outside. The tackle may combo block with the guard or release up for the playside linebacker. If the playside guard is covered inside, head-up, or outside, he must block this defender. If the playside guard is uncovered, he may block down with the center, or release on the playside linebacker.

If not taught correctly, the veer can turn the ball over faster than any play. It has great benefits, but also drawbacks. The quarterback never rides the fullback in the stomach, because this play is very fast. Once he places the ball deep in the fullback's stomach, it becomes the fullback's ball. The quarterback never pitches the ball when a defender is in contact with him. Bad pitches usually occur when the quarterback is off balance.

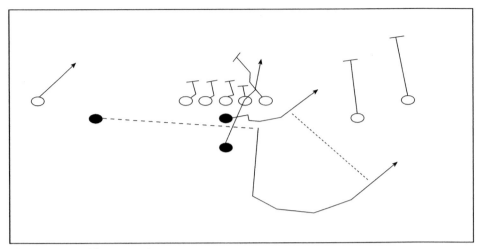

Figure 1-1. Inside veer—Rip 14 In

Pick passes make up the majority of the play-action and dropback passes. (Figure 1-2). Picks allow slower individuals to get open. They also allow the quarterback to have a predetermined route.

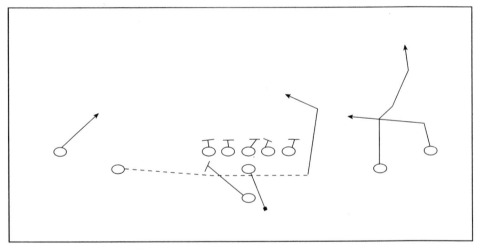

Figure 1-2. Pick—Rip Quick 107

BALANCED FORMATIONS

The spread option offense incorporates balanced formations, motion, and audibles with the inside veer and pick scheme. This dictates strength and attacks weaknesses in opponents' defensive alignments.

The balanced sets consisted of double slots, double twins, double flankers, and double wings. The double slot/twins creates the most pressure on the defense because it forces the defense to align balanced and to play pass or run (Figure 1-3). The number of defenders in the box is an important concept in spread offense. If the defense plays five in the box, you run. If they play six in the box, you can pass or run. If they play seven in the box, you should pass. When using the inside veer and motion into two backs, running against five in the box can be very successful.

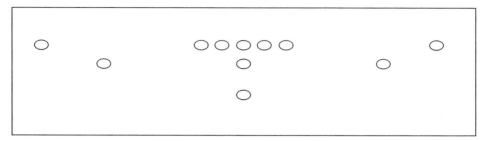

Figure 1-3. Double slot

NFL coach Dick Nolan believed the drawback of four-wide-receiver formations was the limitation of running inside the 20 yard line. Coach Nolan thought that without tight ends it would be difficult to punch it into the end zone. With four wide receivers, the secondary was able to put more pressure on the passing game because the field was smaller. Teams could play tighter man coverage and stuff the run. To overcome this drawback, the spread option offense incorporates a double-flanker formation (Figure 1-4).

In the double-flanker formation, there may be personnel changes with the ends, but the backs stay the same. Even with a smaller end aligned tight, he can veer release and cut block a force defender on the inside veer. Defensive ends forget, or are unable to accomplish their assignments, when the offense continues to jump back and forth in double-slot and double-flanker formations.

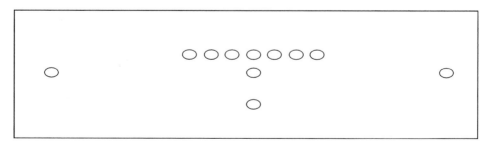

Figure 1-4. Double flanker

MOTION

The use of motion is also an important part of the scheme. With motion the offense can outflank the defense and dictate strength. If a defense rotates the secondary against motion, the free safety, instead of the strong safety, can take on an outside play. Also, many defensive schemes are based on weak and strongside players.

With motion, you have a better idea of the type of secondary coverage being played and these motions can confuse secondary coverage. As soon as you determine the different types of coverage, then you can call certain position or progression reads.

AUDIBLES

Audibles are a big part of this offense. The quarterback can audible to run and passing plays. Many times coaches don't call great plays. You need someone to get you out of a poor decision. That is when the quarterback comes to the rescue. It may be difficult to count on a high school teenager for your team's success, but if you do a good job of teaching, he is like another coach on the field.

The quarterback cannot just audible to any play. He has a few predetermined plays and the situations they are used in. This offense also uses the *Check-With-Me* system, which allows the quarterback to call the direction of the play.

NOT A RUN AND SHOOT

The spread option offense is not a run-and-shoot offense. In the run and shoot, the focus is on routes changing according to coverage and open areas. In the spread option, you only change the routes if the quarterback calls an audible. The backside end opposite the trips receivers is the only read route.

Because many of the routes are progression reads and picks, the quarterback does not have a difficult system of reading coverage. He has a hot receiver, a primary read, and a secondary read. The pick is always the primary read. The offense also uses a couple of position reads that attack the cornerbacks, strong safeties, free safeties, and linebackers.

Some teams automatically change their route combinations according to the coverage. Run-and-shoot teams also run routes to a certain level and decide whether to continue to the next level. spread option offense combinations remain the same because you want to have at least one route out of the four receivers for every coverage. To change a pass combination, the quarterback changes the call on the line of scrimmage.

The run-and-shoot offense requires a lot of time to perfect the reads and levels. The spread option offense needs time to practice the option and traditional power-type plays.

The only type of read route used without an audible is with the backside receiver opposite the trips receivers. This backside receiver can run a slant or fade depending on the backside linebacker and cornerback. This route is very important because it keeps the backside linebacker off the quarterback. spread option also sits down on crossing routes against zone coverage.

TRADITIONAL ATTACK

The spread option offense also incorporates the double-tight and double-wing formations. The flankers or wings are also the backs that motion into two backs or tight-trips sets. If your team wants to get into a power-type game because of personnel, the weather, the game clock, or an opponent's outstanding man coverage versus the double slot, the flanker or wing formation can change the offense into *smash and bash*.

In addition to running the option series out of the double-tight formation, the offense can use traps, leads, counters, powers, and tosses. These strong sets and balanced formations dictate which defensive personnel to attack. When the defense packs it in to stop the run, the play-action passes have more success out of these two formations.

Having a traditional attack also gives you another option if your team is not having success reading the box out of a double-slot formation. Sometimes in a double-slot formation, the offense can get stuffed by a defense using only five in the box. In that situation, bring more bodies into the running area to see if the extra blockers help.

In every offense, there must be screens, draws, and trick plays. These types of plays place tremendous pressure on defenses because it forces them to stay at home and be in control. The trick plays make the defense spend time on something that may or may not be used during a game.

The screens help offensive linemen slow down the defensive rush. Use the screen early in a game to remind the rushers of their responsibilities and force them to slow down. The draws help to keep the linebackers out of the hook zones and prevent them from blitzing outside.

CHAPTER 2

Blueprint

The spread option offense uses a center, two guards, two tackles, a quarterback, and a fullback. The ends (X and Y) can double as tight ends and split ends, while the backs (T and Z) can be slots (Figure 2-1), flankers (Figure 2-2), or wings. You can use all backs in motion. The back positions are interchangeable. The backs and ends must be able to execute their position from either side or direction. If you want the ends and backs to switch sides, call *left* in front of the formation.

X			T G C G T		Y
	T		Q	Z	
			F		

Figure 2-1. Slot personnel

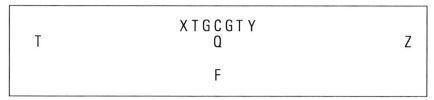

Figure 2-2. Flanker personnel

FORMATIONS

spread option uses four balanced formations: Twins, Slot, Flanker, and Wing (Figures 2-3 through 2-6). The balanced sets pressure the defense to also be balanced. Adding the word *gun* to the front of the formation call places the quarterback four yards back from the center.

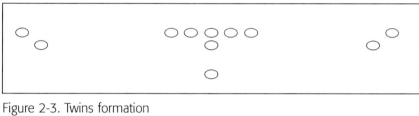

Figure 2-3. Twins formation

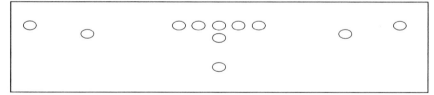

Figure 2-4. Slot formation

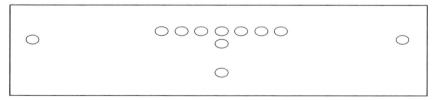

Figure 2-5. Flanker formation

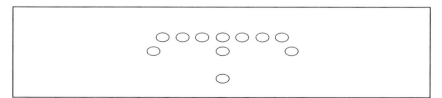

Figure 2-6. Wing formation

MOTION

spread option uses four different types of motion: short, medium, long, and extra-long. All backs (fullback and backs) can be placed in motion. The short motion tells the back to move into a two-back set with the fullback. Keywords determine which side goes into motion. *Roy* or *Lou* tells the backs to use a short motion. To start the back in motion, the quarterback lifts his left leg for the left back or right leg for the right back. *Roy* tells the back on the left side to go in motion to the right behind the fullback, while *Lou* tells the back aligned on the right side to go behind the fullback (Figures 2-7 and 2-8).

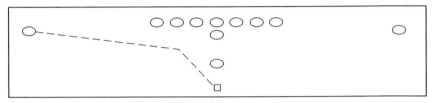

Figure 2-7. Flanker Roy

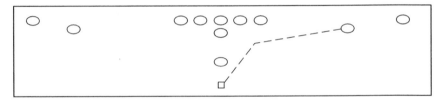

Figure 2-8. Slot Lou

Medium motion is called *Rip* or *Lip*. *Rip* tells the left back to go in motion to the right between the quarterback and fullback. The back stops just past the right tackle or tight end. *Lip* tells the right back to motion to the left and also stop just past the tackle or tight end. To start the back in motion, the quarterback taps his right hip to start the right back and his left hip to start the left back (Figures 2-9 and 2-10).

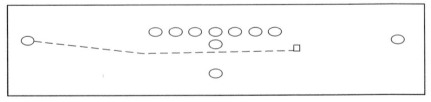

Figure 2-9. Flanker Rip

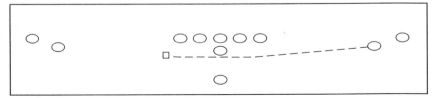

Figure 2-10. Slot Lip

The long motion is called *Larry* or *Reggie*. *Reggie* tells the back on the left side to go in motion between the quarterback and fullback and align between the two receivers on the right side. *Larry* tells the right back to go in motion to the left side and align between the two receivers on the left side (Figures 2-11 and 2-12).

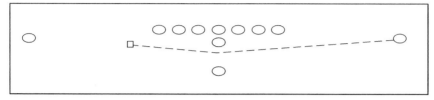

Figure 2-11. Flanker Larry

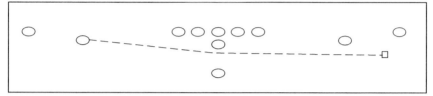

Figure 2-12. Slot Reggie

The extra-long motion sends the back past both receivers to the other side. *Lassie* is the extra-long motion for the right back to the left. *Rover* is the extra-long motion for the left back to the right (Figures 2-13 and 2-14).

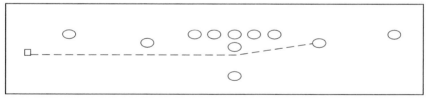

Figure 2-13. Slot Lassie

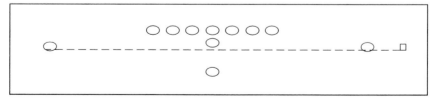

Figure 2-14. Flanker Rover

HOLE ALIGNMENT/GAPS

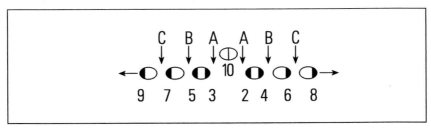

Figure 2-15

The hole alignment uses even numbers to the right and odd numbers to the left. The center has two numbers (*0* to the right hip, and *1* to the left hip.) A, B, and C are the gaps between offensive linemen (Figure 2-15).

The A gap is found between the center and guard. The B gap is between the guard and tackle. The C gap is between the tackle and ends.

The right side of the center is the 0 hole. The inside of the right guard's side is the 2 hole, and the outside hip of the right guard is the 4 hole. Off-tackle to the right side is the 6 hole. The aiming point is the right hip of the tackle. Anything outside the right end is the 8 hole.

The left hip of the center is the 1 hole. The left inside hip of the left guard is the 3 hole. Outside the left guard's hip is the 5 hole. The left tackle's outside hip is the 7 hole (off-tackle). Any play outside to the left is the 9 hole.

RUNNING SERIES – 10'S, 20'S, 40'S, AND 60'S

After the two numbers, running plays are called according to the type of block called in the huddle. These two numbers give the type of running play and direction. The first series is the option. All option plays use the teens (10's) as the first number. The second number determines the hole and also the type of action used. Some of these plays have one, two, and three options. The other plays may only use the option action.

The second running series is designed for the fullback and uses the twenties (20's). These plays are usually run out of one back, except for the trap plays. A consistent throwing team with the fullback as the primary runner will probably use the twenty series most of the time.

The third running series uses a two back set with the short *Roy* and *Lou* motions. This series uses the forties (40's) for the traditional plays from the I Backfield. When you are stronger than your opponents, or the weather conditions are poor for the option, use this attack more often.

The last running series uses the sixties (60's). This tells the tailback (T) and fullback (F) to switch positions. The tailback becomes the primary back-ball carrier. The medium motions, *Rip* and *Lip*, are used for a two-back set. The sixty and the twenty series are almost the same except for the fullback and tailback changing positions.

Option Series – Teens

10 and 11 Mid Line
12 and 13 Base
14 and 15 In
14 OG Right and 15 OG Left
14 and 15 X
14 and 15 G
14 and 15 Belly G
16 and 17 Out
16 and 17 G
16 and 17 Load
18 and 19 Speed
18 and 19 Zone

Fullback Series – Twenties

20 and 21 Trap
22 and 22 Draw
24 and 25 Zone
26 and 27 Power
26 and 27 Counter
28 and 29 Zone
28 and 29 GOG

Motion-Back Series – Forties

40/41/42/43/44 and 45 Lead
42 and 43 Draw
44 and 45 Bounce
46 and 47 Power
26 and 27 Counter
48 and 49 Zone
48 and 49 GOG

Tailback Series – Sixties

60 and 61 Trap
60/61/62/63/64 and 65 Lead
62 and 63 Draw
64 and 65 Zone
64 and 65 Bounce
66 and 67 Power
66 and 67 Counter
68 and 69 Zone
68 and 69 GOG

DROPBACK SERIES – 30'S, 50'S, AND 70'S

Pass plays are called by two different systems. By saying *Quick* (30's), *Stop* (50's), or *Fan* (70's), the offensive line knows how deep the quarterback is going to drop back. The blocking assignments for the offensive line stay the same on these dropback passes. The *Quick*, or 30 Series, is a three-step dropback for the quarterback. The offensive line stays on the line of scrimmage and punch-pass protects. The *Stop,* or 50 Series, is a five-step dropback for the quarterback and the offensive line takes one heel-toe backward step to pass protect. The *Fan,* or 70 Series, is a seven-step drop and the offensive line takes two heel-toe backward steps to pass protect. (Chapter 8 discusses the *Big on Big* pass-protection scheme in detail.) Numbers or letters are added to the call to tell the receivers what routes to run. This scheme is

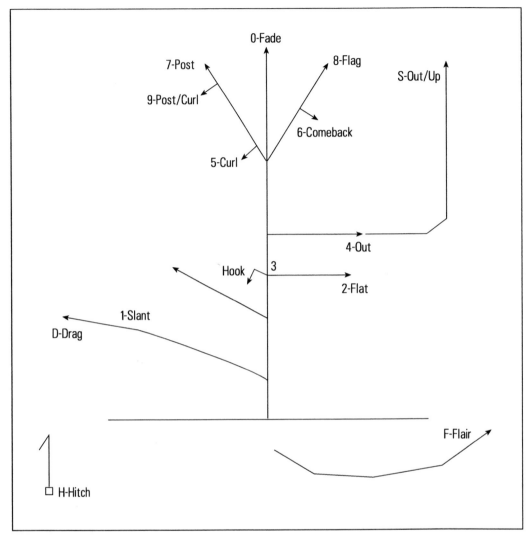

Figure 2-16. Passing tree

very important because it allows the offense to adjust any route combination and to call audibles (Figure 2-16).

With the exception of a *Bootleg,* all passes are called by a series of two, three, or four numbers and/or letters in the huddle. These numbers/letters represent each receiver's route. With the exception of *0,* odd-numbered routes are to the inside. Even-numbered routes are to the outside.

When the quarterback uses a pass audible on the line of scrimmage, he calls out a series: 30's, 50's, or 70's. The following list shows the pass combinations in the dropback series. The number in parentheses indicates the motion man's route in medium, long, or extra-long motion.

Quick – 30 Series	Stop – 50 Series	Fan – 70 Series
30 – Quick 01(2)	54 – Stop 48(3)	76 – Fan 68(5)
31 – Quick 10(7)	55 – Stop 55(0)	77 – Fan 78(4)
32 – Quick 25(0)	57 – Stop 74(D)	78 – Fan 86(C)
33 – Quick 38(F)	58 – Stop 87(2)	79 – Fan 9S(7)
Quick Slant–Go	Stop 48–5D Scoot	
	Stop 5D–48 Scat	

MIRROR ROUTES

After the pass block is called and just two numbers are given without motion, the receivers have mirror routes. The first number tells the outside receiver his route, and the second number tells the inside receiver what route to run. This system stays the same whether the outside receiver is a back or an end. You can call this play *Quick 10* or audible *31*. (Figure 2-17).

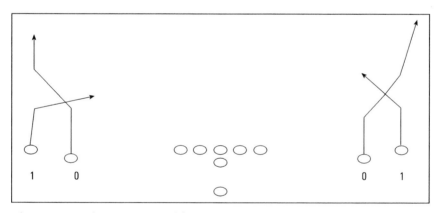

Figure 2-17. Mirror Route—Quick 10 or 31

If four numbers are given in two combinations with no motion, the first two numbers tell the two left receivers their outside and inside routes. The second pair of numbers tells the two right receivers their outside and inside routes. Stop 5D-48 Scat is one example of this kind of play (Figure 2-18).

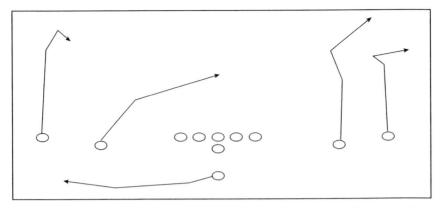

Figure 2-18. Mirror Route—Stop 5D-48 Scat (Left SE - 5, Left Slot - D, Right SE - 4, Right Slot - 8, and FB - Scat)

TRIPS COMBINATIONS

If the call includes motion and three numbers, the route sequence begins with the outside receiver on the trips side. The second number tells the inside receiver what to run and the third number tells the motion man what route to run. If the call does not include a number for the backside split end, he runs a 0 or 1, which is called a Read Route, R. In the 30 Series, this trips-combination route is called 32. All three receivers have to learn the outside, middle, and motion-man routes (Figure 2-19).

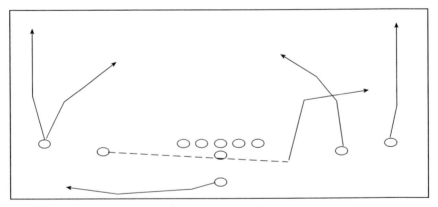

Figure 2-19. Trips combination—Rip - Quick 012 (Right SE - 0, Right Slot - 1, Motion Man - 2, Left SE - Read)

ONE BACK ROUTES

The fullback or tailback can be sent on a pass route by just calling the name of the route at the end of a pass sequence. The one back's routes are Dump, Angle, Delay, Scoot, Shoot, and Scat (Figure 2-20). They can be called to either side.

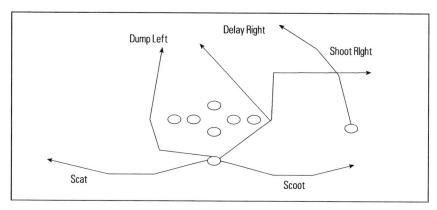

Figure 2-20. One back routes

PLAY-ACTION PASSES

Play-action passes are called by placing the number *1* in front of a running play. The backfield action stays the same, but the offensive line uses an aggressive pass block on the line of scrimmage. The routes will be called at the end of the running play. You can also call an offensive guard (OG) block to help protect the quarterback's blind side. On bootleg passes, the receivers run a levels-sequence-route combination. *Levels* tells the widest playside receiver to run an 8 route. If you have a second playside receiver, he runs a 4 route. If the fullback is not making a fake, he runs a shoot route playside and the backside receivers drag and post. Use an OG block on all bootlegs. See Figures 2-21 and 2-22 for examples of play-action passes.

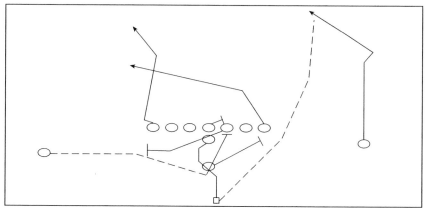

Figure 2-21. Play-action pass Roy—1 - 44 - 7D8 (Right Flanker - 7, Right TE - D, and Left TE - 8)

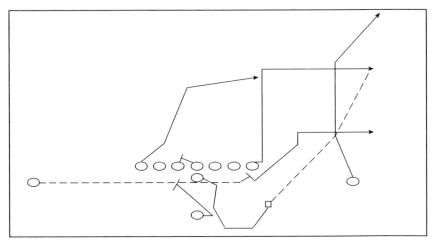

Figure 2-22. Play-action pass Rip—67 Bootleg Right (Right Flanker - 8, Right TE - 4, Left TE - D, FB - Shoot)

CADENCE

When the quarterback comes to the line of scrimmage, he first yells, "Down." "Down" tells everyone to get ready to start the play and tells the offensive line to be in a three-point stance. The only time the offensive line is in a two-point stance is in the *gun* formation. The quarterback yells two different combinations of numbers, for example, "14-54." He then repeats the same sequence, "14-54." These numbers come from the different offensive series. As he calls out the numbers, he lifts his leg or pats his hip. After the motion back reaches his position, the quarterback yells "Ready!" then "Set!" If the ball is not snapped on "Set," then the quarterback yells "Go!" The ball is usually snapped on "Set." However, you should use "Go" at least a quarter of the time to keep the defense honest. The full cadence for this example is "Down, 14-54, 14-54, Ready, Set, Go."

AUDIBLES

The audible system in spread option offense was created to take advantage of the number of defenders in the box, attack particular defensive personnel, and attack unbalanced alignments. The system uses both running and passing audibles and a number series of two combinations (instead of colors) to call the audibles.

When the quarterback comes to the line of scrimmage, he counts the number of safeties. If he has zero safeties, he may audible to a pass. If he has two safeties, he may audible to a running play using any of his three backs. When he has only one safety, he can change the direction of the play called, audible to a to a different pass or run, or wait for the motion and run the play called. In certain situations the quarterback must stay with the pass or run play called in the huddle, but he can still change the pass routes and the type or direction of the run play.

In the cadence, the quarterback calls out two numbers. If the first number is the same play called in the huddle, he is changing the play to the second number in the sequence. For example, if the play in the huddle was called "14 in" and the quarterback yells out "14-31, 14-31," he just changed the running play to a three-step pass.

If the play in the huddle was a four- or three-route combination, the quarterback can still call out just the first two numbers of the pass combination to change the call or yell "check" after the sequence to alert the offense of his intentions. For example, if the play was "5D-48 Scat," and the defense shifts into a two deep secondary with five in the box on second down and long, the quarterback audibles to a fullback draw by yelling "check, Check, 53-22, 53-22." "Check, check" overrides any play called. Giving two sets of numbers ensures that the defense will not understand the change. The number of running and passing audibles should be limited at first. The running audibles should consist of 14/15 in, 18/19 Speed, and 22/23 Draw. The passing audibles should consist of 30, 31, 54, and 57. Remember, each of these combinations can be mirror routes with short or no motion and trips combinations with medium, long, and extra-long motion. Depending on your team's offensive personnel, these could be the only audibles used during the entire season. For each week, the offense may game plan certain audibles they believe will be successful.

See Figures 2-23 through 2-25 for examples of running, passing, and strength-change situations.

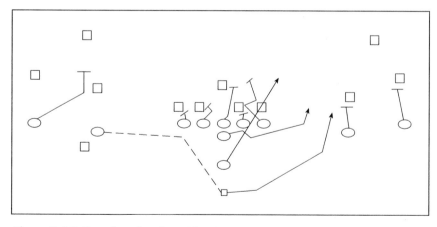

Figure 2-23. Running situation—57-14, 57-14

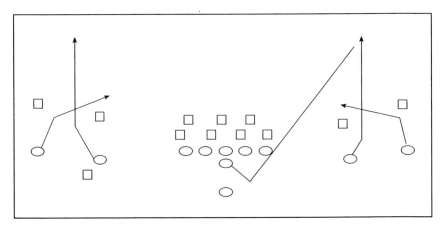

Figure 2-24. Passing situation—14-31, 14-31

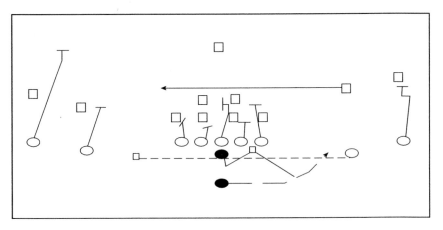

Figure 2-25. Strength-change situation—62-18, 62-18

80 SERIES

The 80 Series is a goal line Check-With-Me. This series generally uses a double-wing formation. The quarterback has the option to call lead, power, or toss. He can also call a play-action pass. The following list shows the goal line check-with-me series:

80 – Power-Pass Right

81 – Power-Pass Left

82-85 – Lead

86/87 – Power

88/89 – Zone Toss

90 SERIES

The 90 Series is a slot Check-With-Me that allows the quarterback to call the inside veer, draw, quick passes, stop passes, and speed option. The 90 Series enables the quarterback to count the safeties and gives the offense a different set of audibles for the same play. The slot Check-With-Me series consists of the following plays:

90 – Quick 01	94/95 – Inside Veer
91 – Quick 10	96 – Stop 68
92/93 – Draw	97 – Stop 74
	98/99 – Speed Option

SCREENS, REVERSES, AND SPECIAL PLAYS

Besides running and passing plays, the offense includes screens, reverses, and special plays. Screens are very important for slowing down a strong pass rush. The screen package includes middle screens, right and left screens, hitch passes, and double-quick screens. On the middle screens, you will generally use the fullback. The right/left screens offer two options: using either the tight end or fullback out of the double-tight formations. The split ends are used for the hitch passes and quick screens to either side.

The screen is a great second and long play. Because it is a higher percentage play, it reminds the defensive line to slow down on their rush. The screen is a great equalizer for an aggressive defensive front and quick dropping linebackers.

The offense also keeps the defense honest with reverses. The reverses are called off the toss action. You can use the fullback, backs, and ends in the reverses. All the formations have some type of reverse. When a defense is attacking the ball and not staying at home, one reverse can help keep those cutback lanes open.

The special plays consist of a double pass, fullback pass, reverse pass, and wrap-around. You should practice one or two trick plays for each game. The special plays help to keep the defense honest and keep the offense exciting.

CHAPTER 3

Secondary

Reading the secondary is very important to any offense. Before the quarterback can audible, he needs to learn the different types of secondary coverages he will see with the double-slot and flanker formations. With any of the base formations, the secondary can play three basic types of balanced coverages. The defense must decide whether it wants to play pass, run, or attack strong.

0 - 1 - 2 RULE

Reading the box is a huge part of this offense. Instead of counting the defenders in the box, count the number of safeties. If the defense has no safeties and is playing man cross, *zero* tells the quarterback to pass. *Two* tells the quarterback that the defense has two safeties, which creates a better chance to run the ball. If the defense has only one safety, the quarterback can look to pass, but can still run. The quarterback can also elect to wait for the defense's reaction to motion before making a decision. It does not matter if the offensive formation is slot or flanker, but defenses tend to have trouble with the double-slot/twins formation in making a decision which direction to take.

COVER ZERO

The first coverage is zero. Zero coverage does not have a free safety. The defense is playing seven in the box against the slot formation. This is a strong passing situation (Figure 3-1).

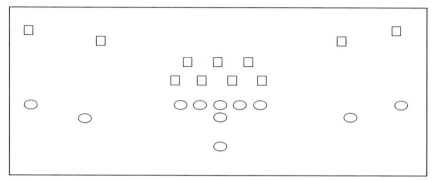

Figure 3-1. Cover zero

Motion forces the secondary to make adjustments. The secondary may rotate into a free safety or stay in a man-to-man coverage. In *man* or *rotate* the secondary can play combos, zone, or stay man (Figures 3-2 and 3-3).

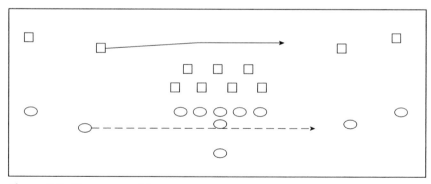

Figure 3-2. Cover zero—Man

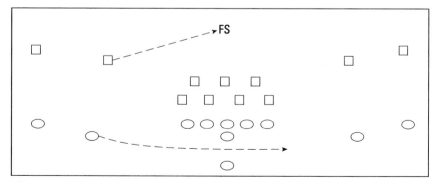

Figure 3-3. Cover zero—Rotate

COVER 2

The second coverage is called 2. When the secondary uses two safeties, it places five in the box against the slot formation, or seven in the box against the flanker formation. This is usually a good running situation, especially with short motion and a run to the strongside .

Passing becomes more difficult because of the extra defender in a two-deep coverage. The one advantage of passing the ball against cover 2 is the lack of a pass rush. The offensive line and fullback should have all the pass rushers blocked. This should give the quarterback more time to find the uncovered receiver. Without motion, it is difficult to tell if the cover 2 is a zone or man (Figure 3-4).

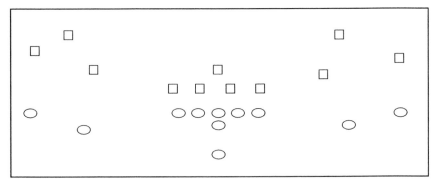

Figure 3-4. Cover 2

When motion occurs, cover 2 can respond in different ways. They can play zone, man, or rotate. In Two Zone, the secondary stays in their area position, but the backside backer can still blitz or drop back into the coverage versus the motion. On the strongside, the coverage is probably a zone of some type, but it still allows a strong throw because they have three defenders versus three receivers (Figure 3-5).

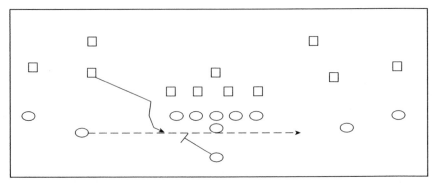

Figure 3-5. Cover 2—Zone

In Two Man, a defender will run across the formation with the motion man. Any defender who runs across the alignment with the motion man is called *Unwelcome Stranger*. On rotate, the playside safety rotates down to take an area or a man. All of these coverages have different versions of combinations and blitzes (Figures 3-6 through 3-8).

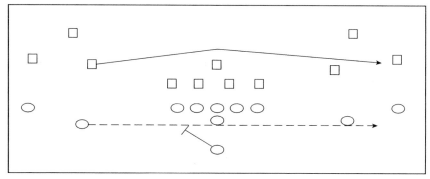

Figure 3-6. Cover 2—Man (Double Slot)

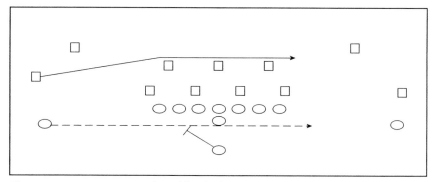

Figure 3-7. Cover 2—Man (Double Flanker)

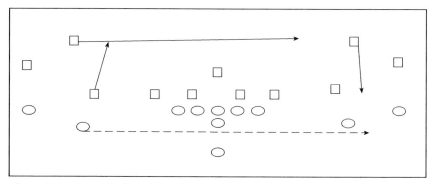

Figure 3-8. Cover 2—Rotate

COVER 1

The last type of secondary coverage is cover 1 (Figure 3-9). *1* is one safety. He aligns deep in the middle of the field. Cover 1 can be a zone, man, or rotate coverage, or a combination of zone or man. When a secondary aligns in this coverage, you want to pass, but also look to run depending on the defense's alignment.

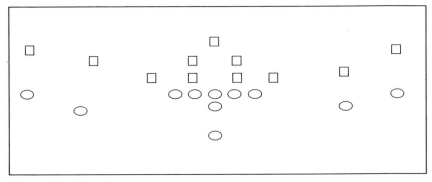

Figure 3-9. Cover 1

In cover 1, the reaction to medium, long, or extra-long motion can be man, zone, or rotate (Figures 3-10 through 3-12).

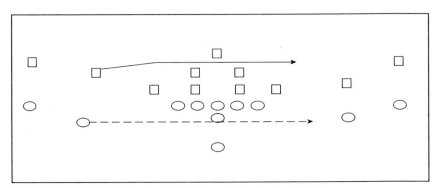

Figure 3-10. Cover 1—Man

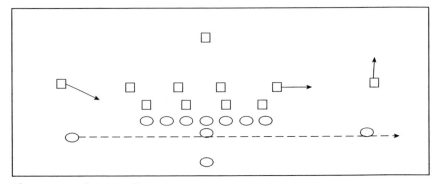

Figure 3-11. Cover 1—Zone

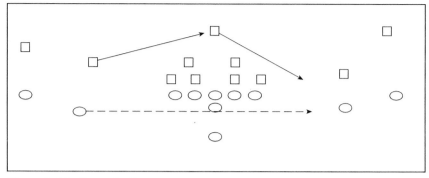

Figure 3-12. Cover 1—Rotate

UNBALANCED SECONDARY

If the defense does not align balanced when you are in any of the double formations, attack the weakside with the pass or run and do not use motion. In this situation, the secondary can be in zero, 1, or 2. The audible can be an automatic dump pass to the uncovered player or some type of option (Figures 3-13 and 3-14).

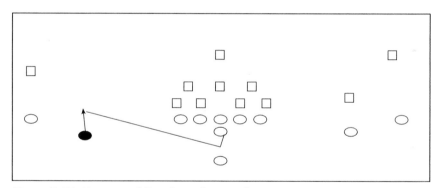

Figure 3-13. Uncovered Receiver—Automatic

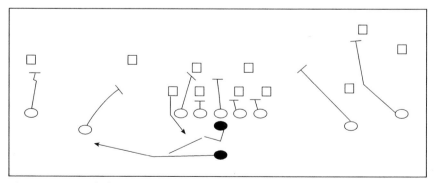

Figure 3-14. Unbalanced secondary—19

WHO'S OPEN?

Once the quarterback learns the basic secondary coverages, he can follow some general passing rules. The quarterback should have predetermined areas of attack for each coverage. Before the snap, he must know if any of the particular routes in the combination have a better chance to be open. In the presnap read, if the called routes do not look good, the quarterback should change the routes or the play. The following is a list of coverages and how to attack each one:

Zero coverage (no motion) should be attacked by routes that open quickly (fades, slants, hooks, bubbles, dumps, scats, and scoots). This coverage usually has some type of uncovered blitz. The quarterback should throw the ball by his first or second step, unless the linebackers are off the line of scrimmage (Figure 3-15).

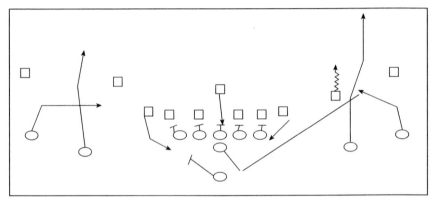

Figure 3-15. Zero coverage (no motion)—Quick 10

Zero-man coverage against motion can be hurt on the backside with the slant, or playside quick routes (fades, slants, flats, bubbles, dumps, and hitches). Zero-man coverage also tends to rush seven defenders against the slot/twin formation. The quarterback must take only a one- or two-step drop, while the offensive line should use the chop block for the quick pass (Figure 3-16).

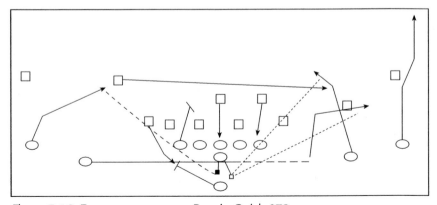

Figure 3-16. Zero-man coverage—Reggie Quick 072

You can attack zero-rotate coverage with three- and five-step routes. The backside or playside quick routes such as slants, dumps, bubbles, outs, flags, and posts are good (Figure 3-17).

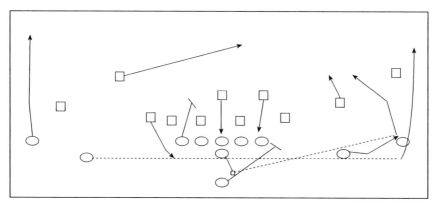

Figure 3-17. Zero-rotate coverage—Quick 1FO

One coverage (no motion) should read the outside and seam routes. Depending on how tight the coverage is playing, these routes can be short, middle, and deep. The outs, fades, slants, flags, drags, curls, and bootlegs will hurt this coverage. Against the slot and twin formations, this defense is only rushing six, so every defender in the box should be blocked (Figure 3-18).

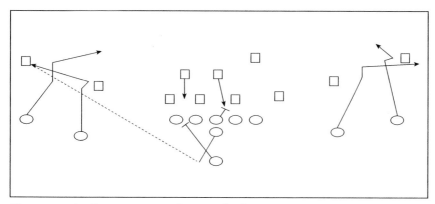

Figure 3-18. One coverage (no motion)—Stop 74

One-man coverage (motion) should be attacked on the backside with crossing routes and weakside running plays. Call routes towards the three-receiver side, but there will be an extra defender (Figure 3-19).

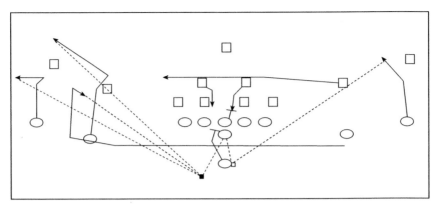

Figure 3-19. One-man coverage (motion) Larry—Stop 483

Against one-man coverage, you should usually audible to the pass, but weakside running plays away from the trips formation can also be a productive play because that flank does not have a defender on it (Figure 3-20).

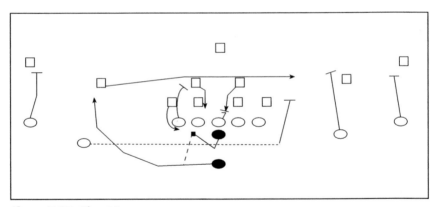

Figure 3-20. Rip—19

One-zone coverage (motion) has a weakness to the motion side, but there can also be backside pressure. The quarterback can counter with a backside slant, but he should still have all defenders blocked. The outs, flags, curls, dumps, seams, and bubbles can hurt this coverage (Figure 3-21).

One-rotate coverage is similar to one-man coverage. Against the slot, the defense only has six players to rush. Against the flanker formation, the defense can rush eight. It will be more difficult to throw to the motion side because of the extra defender. The bootleg, drags, backside post, and backside routes are good routes to use (Figure 3-22).

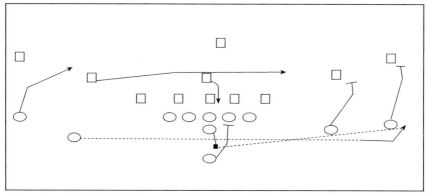

Figure 3-21. One-zone coverage (motion) Reggie—Quick BBF

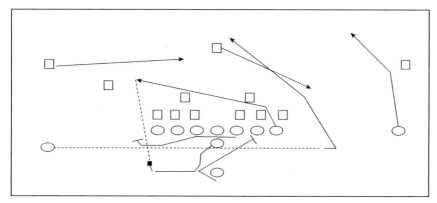

Figure 3-22. One-rotate coverage Flanker Reggie 66 Bootleg

Two coverage (no motion) is more difficult to pass against, but not impossible. The middle of the coverage is the best area to hit an open receiver. The dumps, seams, drags, curls, digs, post curl, and comeback routes are good. The major problem is not knowing if the coverage is zone or man. The best way to attack cover 2 is to run (Figure 3-23).

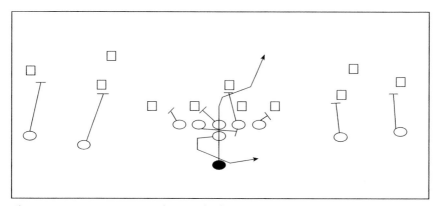

Figure 3-23. Two coverage (no motion)—20 Trap

To throw against cover 2, the quarterback needs to attack the middle. The curls, digs, comebacks, middle screens, post curls, and crossing routes can be effective (Figure 3-24).

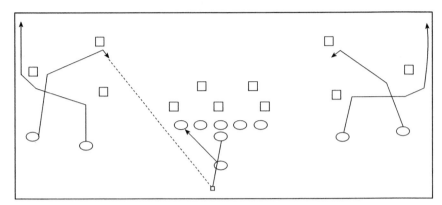

Figure 3-24. Fan 9S

Two-man and two-rotate coverage (motion) can be attacked on the backside using crossing routes, slants, post curl, and fullback routes. This coverage may also blitz the backside linebacker, so there may be slants and fullback swings to the backside. If the secondary over-rotates with extra-long motion, the drags and over the middle posts from the strongside are good routes (Figure 3-25).

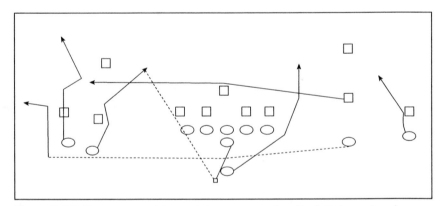

Figure 3-25. Two-man and two-rotate coverage (motion) Twins – Lassie – Stop 872 Dump

Two-zone weakness is the three-receiver formation versus motion. Two defenders will be in the flat and hook area with one deep. The backside receiver is outnumbered, but the frontside receivers have 3-on-3. These three receivers attempt to sit down in the open areas. Even though it is a zone, you can still have success with picks. If the backside linebacker blitzes, the fullback should be able to block him (Figure 3-26).

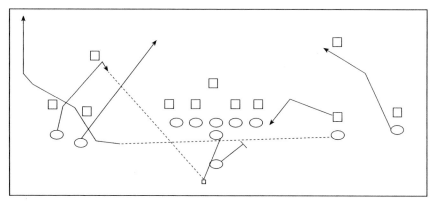

Figure 3-26. Two Zone Twins—Lip—Fan 97S

CHAPTER 4

Audibles (0 - 1 - 2 Rule)

The two base schemes for the spread option offense are the inside veer and picks/crossing routes. With a flexible audible system, these items can take advantage of weaknesses in the defensive alignment and personnel. Aligning in a four-receiver formation at the beginning of each play forces certain decisions. The defense must ask, "Do I play run or pass?" When the offense aligns in double slot, double twins, and even double flanker, the defense can go in different directions. When the offense aligns in the double-wing formation, the defense will probably *pack it in* and try to stuff the offense.

Chapter 3 discussed the different types of secondary coverage(s) and what types of plays would take advantage of their alignments. This chapter goes into more detail concerning the audibles made on the line of scrimmage.

SLOT/TWIN VS. FLANKER/WING

The 0-1-2 Rule can be applied to any formation, but it works best in the double-slot/twin formation. If you have to run or pass, you want as few defenders in the area as possible so you will have fewer blocks to make and fewer secondary defenders to read.

You can still look to audible in the flanker/wing power formations, but the pass may be more of a game planned play-action pass. For example, if you called "Flanker - Roy -14 In," but the defense was tight on the line of scrimmage, the quarterback could audible to "14-Dump, 14-Dump." This is a dump pass to the playside tight end. Or, if on first down, you called "Flanker - 54," the quarterback could call out, "54-20, 54-20," to change the play to a trap with the fullback. On audibles, do not change formations from slot/twin to flanker/wing, or from flanker/wing to slot/twin.

ZERO RULE

As discussed in Chapter 3, zero coverage tells the quarterback to check to pass plays. Once the quarterback determines the coverage is zero, he needs to know the depth of the four secondary defenders and linebackers. The depth will help determine the route combinations.

Tight Secondary and Tight Linebackers

If the safeties and linebackers are tight, *30* can be called in the slot or twin formation (Figure 4-1). The offensive line cut blocks because the quarterback only takes one or two steps back. The presnap read is the seam/slant route by the second receiver or the first receiver's fade. The quarterback must throw quickly because there will be a defender rushing.

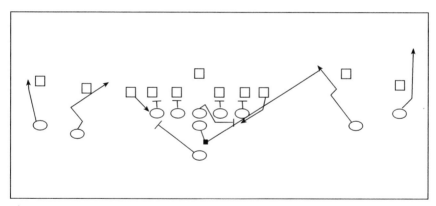

Figure 4-1. 30

If the safeties are playing off, the quarterback could audible to *31* (Figure 4-2). The split end runs a slant under the back's fade. The quarterback takes only one or two steps back because of the pressure. The slant should be open. If the safety is jumping the slant, the quarterback can throw the fade, or call *30*.

If the formation is double flanker and the safeties and linebackers are tight, the quarterback can audible to any outside route for the backs and keep the tight ends in to block by saying the letter *B* after the series. For example, the quarterback could call, "57B" (Figure 4-3). This tells the backs to run the *7* routes (Posts) and the tight ends to block.

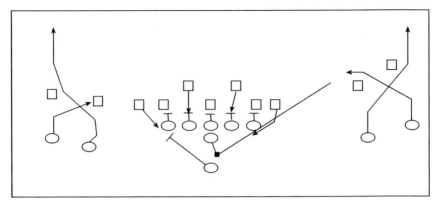

Figure 4-2. 31

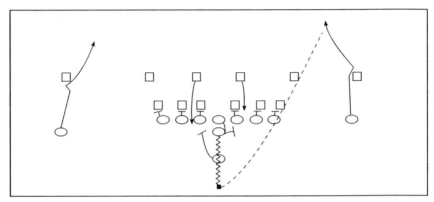

Figure 4-3. 30

Tight Secondary and Deep Linebackers

If the secondary is in a tight-zero coverage, but the linebackers are playing deep, the quarterback should be able to throw a Stop series route (five-step pass) before the backers could reach the quarterback on a delay fire. The key for calling a five-step dropback pass is the quarterback knowing that only six or fewer defenders can get to him. The middle should be attacked with a 57 (Figure 4-4). The outside receivers run posts and the inside receivers run underneath 4 routes (outs). If the safeties are deep, the quarterback can throw to the out.

If the linebackers are off and the four defenders are playing a quarter combo coverage where they switch if the receivers cross, run the 54 (Figure 4-5). In 54, the outside receiver runs the out and the inside receiver runs a flag. The quarterback makes a position read on the cornerback. If the corner jumps the out (4), he throws deep to the flag (8). If the corner drops deep to cover his quarter, the quarterback throws the out. Remember that against slot, the defense cannot run a seven-man rush against a five-step drop because it has only six blockers.

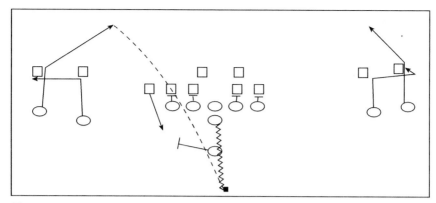

Figure 4-4. 57

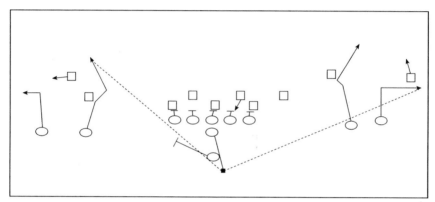

Figure 4-5. 54

Zero Coverage Vs. Trips

The quarterback can also call for a medium, long, or extra-long motion to three receivers against zero coverage. He must know the number of rushers and whether the secondary rotates into 1 coverage. Usually the backside slant is open, unless the backside linebacker is back to take the slant away. If this occurs, the trips receiver side is the read.

The motion back, the third receiver in the trips formation, will have a complementary route that goes with the outside receiver's route. For example, on 30, the motion back runs a 2 route from medium motion underneath the 1 pick route (Figure 4-6).

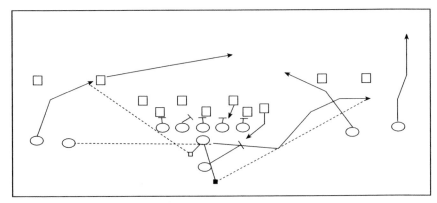

Figure 4-6. 30

TWO RULE

In a 2 coverage, the defense is playing pass. On first and second downs, the quarterback needs to run inside and off tackle. When the offense aligns in a double-twin or slot formation, there will be five defenders near the line of scrimmage. The quarterback can call for a running play with or without motion. If he does use motion, he will usually run to the strongside towards motion.

Three-man Front

If the defense is playing a 50 alignment with a three-man front, the quarterback has different options. He should know the defensive tackles are protecting their outside. On a 4i technique, the defensive tackle may slant inside to the B gap with the playside backer looping outside. The quarterback should also know what side the defensive noseguard is playing and look for any linebacker blitz. With no motion, he can audible to a trap, draw, base, or X (Figures 4-7 through 4-10).

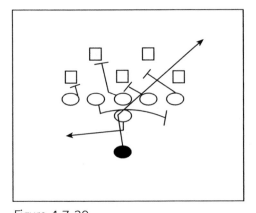

Figure 4-7. 20

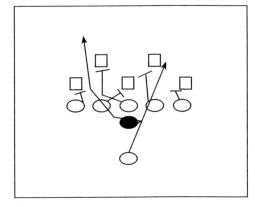

Figure 4-8. 14X

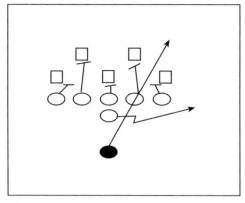

Figure 4-9. 24

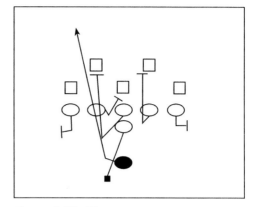

Figure 4-10. 23

With motion, the inside veer is your first choice. But you can still run the lead, trap, midline option, speed option, power, and counter (Figures 4-11 through 4-14). You should game plan these other running plays, as well as the inside veer.

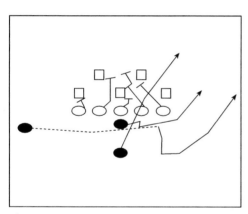

Figure 4-11. 14

Figure 4-12. 42

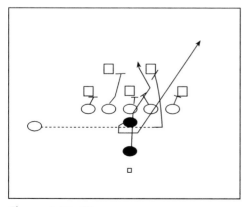

Figure 4-13. 10

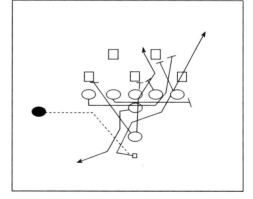

Figure 4-14. 46C

When the defense has five down linemen and two linebackers versus the double-flanker formation, it is more difficult to run because more blocks have to be made. But if you're not having success against five in the box, you may elect to use the double-flanker formation because the defenders on the tight ends are probably playing pass. Send your ends to block down, out, or hook, and their defenders will probably follow. The flanker formation can provide better blocking angles (Figures 4-15 and 4-16).

The quarterback may audible to counters, options, powers, tosses, or any other running play game planned for the week. The runs should be towards motion to outnumber the defense to that side. Before deciding which gaps to run, the quarterback needs to check the positions of the defensive tackles and noseguard.

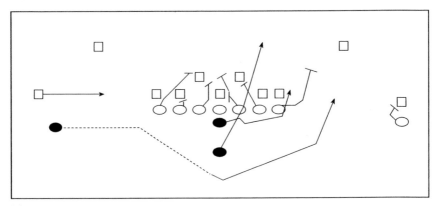

Figure 4-15. 14

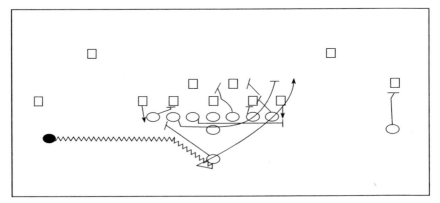

Figure 4-16. 46C

Four-man Front

When the defense is playing a four-man front with six defensive backs and a middle linebacker, the quarterback has several options. With no motion, the trap, draw, line and counter options should have success. If the defensive tackles are playing head-up or outside, the trap is a good audible. If the defensive tackles are pinching, line and counter options are also good (Figures 4-17 through 4-20).

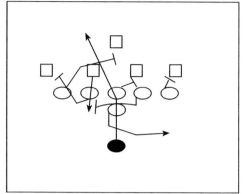

Figure 4-17. 21

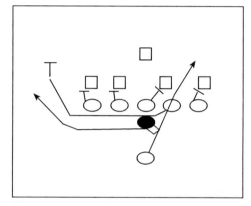

Figure 4-18. 10

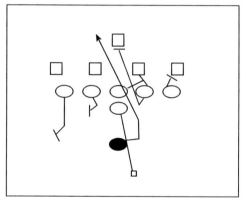

Figure 4-19. 22

Figure 4-20. 14 OG

With motion, the defense can react in different ways. Usually when you motion into the I formation, the defender over the motion man stays on his side. The front may shift or slant towards motion, but the defender stays on the weakside (Figure 4-21).

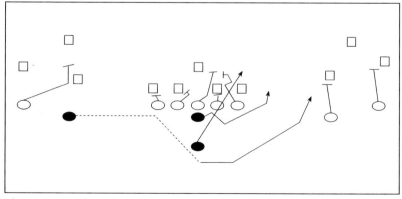

Figure 4-21. 14

With short and medium motion, run towards the motion side because the defense is outnumbered. The base play to call is still the inside veer 14/15. You can game plan for other plays out of two backs, but this double-team to the middle backer is the best chance. The quarterback must be ready to run the alleys if he keeps the ball. (See Figures 4-22 and 4-23 for more two back running plays to game plan.)

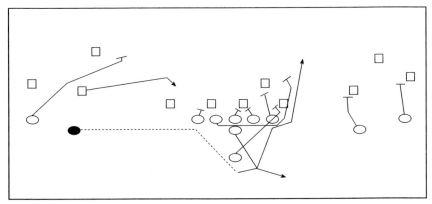

Figure 4-22. 46P

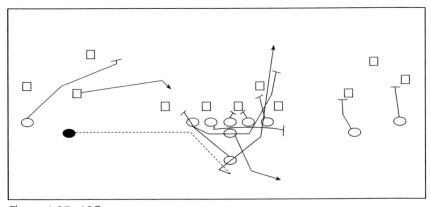

Figure 4-23. 46C

If the defense is playing a 2 coverage versus the double-flanker formation, you can still audible to running plays. The man coverage on the tight ends allows these defenders to be blocked. The outside linebackers covering the tight ends tend to get hooked, kicked-out, and loaded because their concern is to not allow the tight ends to catch the ball. Without motion, the counters and line option could have success (Figures 4-24 and 4-25).

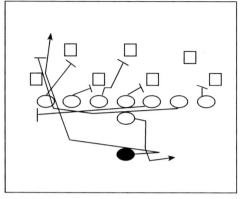

Figure 4-24. 27C

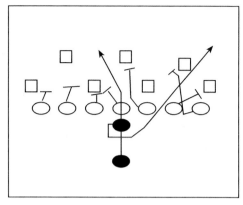

Figure 4-25. 10

The game plan is different when using short motion for a two-back set. You can run toss, counter, lead, and the inside veer (Figures 4-26 through 4-29).

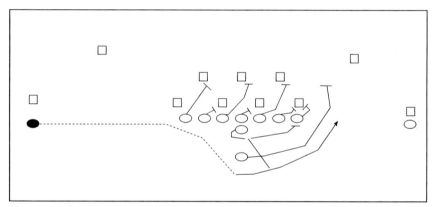

Figure 4-26. 48

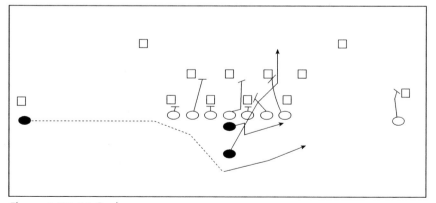

Figure 4-27. 14 Seal

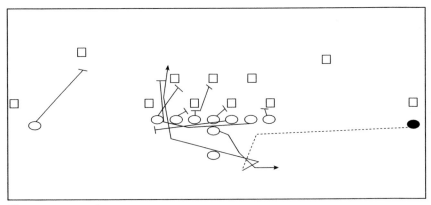

Figure 4-28. 47C

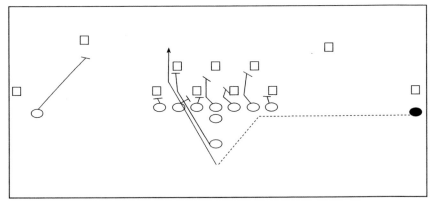

Figure 4-29. 45

ONE RULE

One coverage is when the defense elects to keep one man deep over the middle. This will place six defenders in the box against a double-slot/twins formation, or eight defenders in the box versus a double-flanker formation. When the quarterback sees this coverage, he must check the following progression.

Unbalanced Defensive Alignment

When the offense aligns in a balanced formation, and the defense aligns more defenders to the left or right side, the quarterback can pass or run to the weakside . The quarterback does not count the defender over the center (middle linebacker or noseguard) or the free safety in the middle. There will be five defenders on one side and four defenders on the other side. Pass or run to the side of the four defenders.

When the quarterback walks up to the line of scrimmage, he first checks for uncovered receivers. Audible to a pass if one of the receivers is uncovered. Play 57 or 54 will take advantage of this situation, unless the defense is rushing seven. In that case, the quarterback needs to audible to 30 or 31.

The quarterback can also run the ball to the four-man side because of the extra blocker. Speed option, counter weak, or toss can have success in this situation (Figures 4-30 through 4-32).

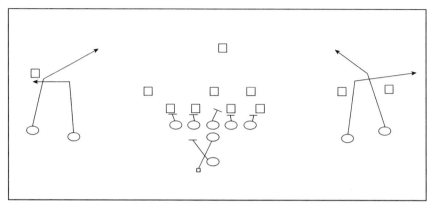

Figure 4-30. 57—Progression read

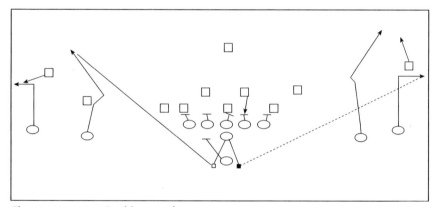

Figure 4-31. 54—Position read

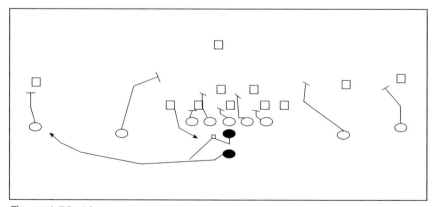

Figure 4-32. 19

Shifting Defenses

When the offense motions short or long, and the defense shifts out of a coverage or leaves a receiver uncovered, the quarterback can still check to another audible to counter this shift. The quarterback can run or pass depending on what the defense leaves open. For example, if the offense called Roy-14, but the playside defender covering the slot comes off to help stop the run, the quarterback can receive a silent snap and throw an automatic pass (Figure 4-33).

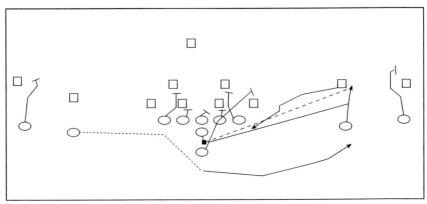

Figure 4-33. Automatic pass

Cover 1 Man or Rotate

When a defender comes across the formation with the motion man, the defense becomes a man or rotate type of coverage. This is called an *Unwelcome Stranger*. With medium, long, and extra-long motion, the quarterback can attack the weakside with pass or run because of the lack of defenders. For running plays, the quarterback can call speed option, counters, and tosses. Backside slants and bootlegs are good passes against this coverage (Figures 4-34 and 4-35).

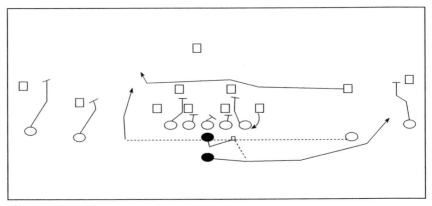

Figure 4-34. 18

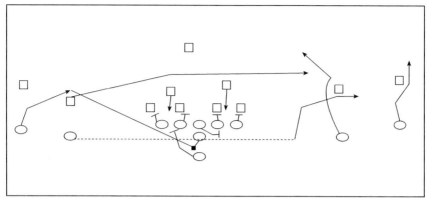

Figure 4-35. 30—Backside vs. Unwelcome Stranger

When using short motion (Roy/Lou), the quarterback can still run or pass to the strongside against man coverage because the backside defender usually stays. The offense has the advantage because of numbers. The inside veer, toss, counters, or other running plays can be game planned for the week (Figures 4-36 and 4-37).

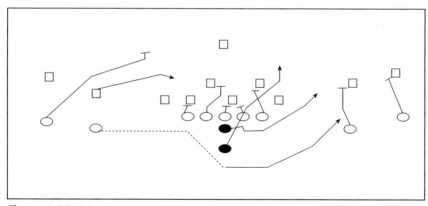

Figure 4-36. 14

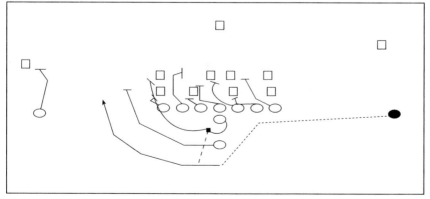

Figure 4-37. 49

The passes out of the two-back set can be picks or position reads to the strongside. The motion man that comes into the two-back set can block to the strongside as the fullback blocks to the weakside. Versus cover 1, the backside receiver can run a read route, or the first number of the mirror combination, because the offense should have every rusher blocked. Figures 4-38 and 4-39 illustrate two routes that could hurt one-man coverage to the strongside.

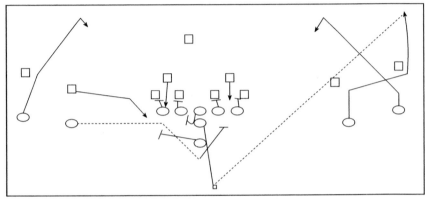

Figure 4-38. 79—Position/progressio

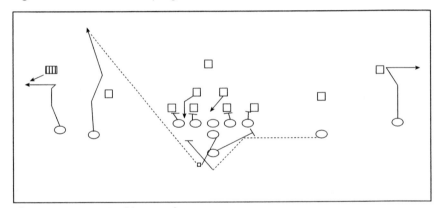

Figure 4-39. 54—Position read

Cover 1 Zone

Cover 1 zone is a three-deep coverage that does not rotate over motion. This coverage allows the offense to outflank the defense with motion. Passes and runs can be effective to the strongside. Figures 4-40 and 4-41 illustrate examples of two pass plays against cover 1 zone.

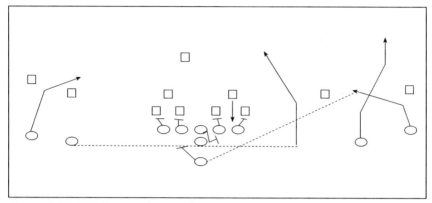

Figure 4-40. 31—Progression read

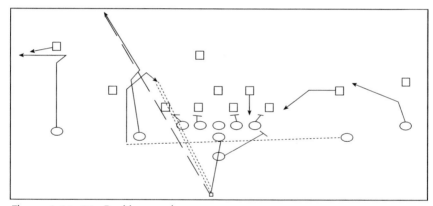

Figure 4-41. 54—Position read

The inside veer is the play of choice, but you can also game plan variations of the inside veer, such as 14/15 G and 16/17 Outside Veer (Figures 4-42 and 4-43).

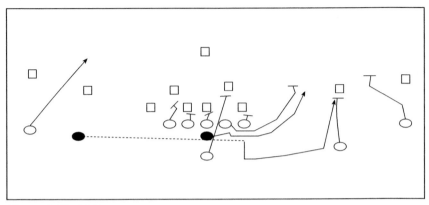

Figure 4-42. 14G

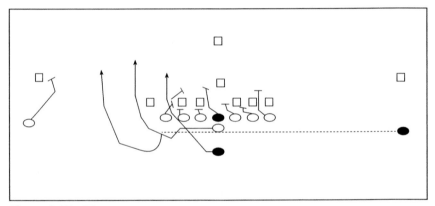

Figure 4-43. 17

CHAPTER 5

Blocks and Schemes

In the spread option offense, every play has some type of key block that is called with the play. This chapter discusses these blocks and schemes in detail. The subsequent chapters include diagrams of all the plays in each series.

BASE

Base is a drive-blocking rule that gives the offensive line a numbering-rule system. The defensive lineman or linebacker over, or inside the center, is 0. The next defensive lineman or linebacker is P1. The third defender on or off the line of scrimmage is P2. The last defender on the line of scrimmage is P3. The strong safety or force man is P4. The center drive blocks 0 away from the hole, the playside guard drive blocks P1 away from the hole, the playside tackle drive blocks P2, and the playside tight end drive blocks P3 away from the hole. The backside guard and tackle base block B1 and B2. If P1 is stacked behind a defensive tackle (P2), the playside guard must combo block with the playside tackle. Figures 5-1 through 5-3 illustrate the blocking schemes for 12 Base, 22 Base, and 62 Base.

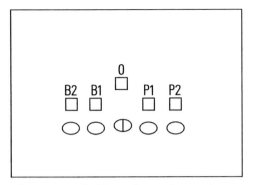

Figure 5-1. Blocking scheme for 12 Base

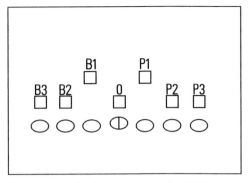

Figure 5-2. Blocking scheme for 22 Base

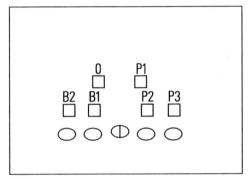

Figure 5-3. Blocking scheme for 62 Base

BELLY

Belly tells the playside tackle to block down on a covered playside guard, and tells the playside guard to pull behind for a kick-out or roll block on the first defender in front or past the playside tackle. If the playside tackle is covered, he hook blocks that defender. If the formation is using a tight end, the guard will block the force man because the playside tight end hook blocks the defensive end. The fullback will block the strongside linebacker. Backside linemen block base. Figures 5-4 through 5-6 illustrate three variations of 14 Belly.

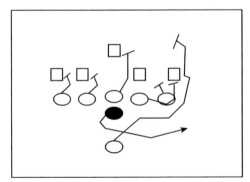

Figure 5-4. 14 Belly—Variation A

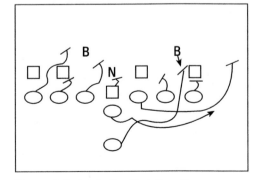

Figure 5-5. 14 Belly—Variation B

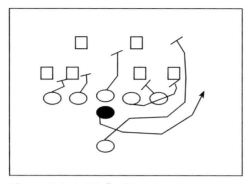

Figure 5-6. 14 Belly—Variation C

BIG ON BIG

Big on Big is the blocking scheme for Quick, Stop, and Fan. The covered linemen block their defender. If a lineman is uncovered, he checks for a blitzing linebacker directly in front as he helps his partner double-team. If the defensive line stacks two middle linebackers over the guards, the center always takes the linebacker to the right and the fullback takes the linebacker to the left.

Before the snap, the fullback checks for linebackers stacked in the middle and then checks for any outside linebacker. The fullback can always walk up into the left A gap if the linebacker steps up to threaten the line of scrimmage. Figures 5-7 through 5-10 illustrate four examples of Big on Big.

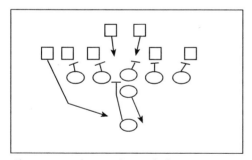

Figure 5-7. Big on Big—Variation A

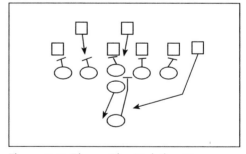

Figure 5-8. Big on Big—Variation B

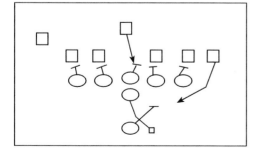

Figure 5-9. 14 Big on Big—Variation C

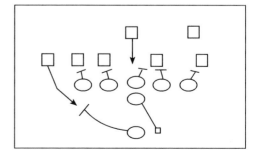

Figure 5-10. Big on Big—Variation D

BOUNCE

Bounce tells the playside guard, tackle, and tight end to take one base step playside in order to sell the lead, but then hook block their defenders (defensive lineman or linebacker playing directly in front of them) to the inside. The running back automatically bounces to the outside. The fullback takes two steps downhill towards the playside tackle's inside leg, but then breaks around the end to seal block on the linebacker. Figures 5-11 through 5-13 illustrate the playside blocking for 44 and 64 Bounce.

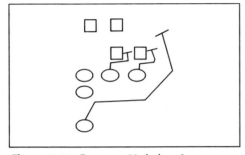

Figure 5-11. Bounce—Variation A

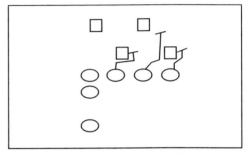

Figure 5-12. Bounce—Variation B

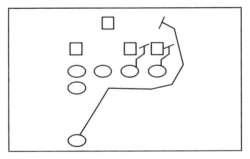

Figure 5-13. Bounce—Variation C

CLIMB

Climb tells the fullback on the lead-running play to place his facemask between the numbers of a linebacker stepping into the running lane. Once the fullback is at the impact location, he tries to climb up the defender. Do not cut the defender and leave him in the hole.

CHOP

Chop tells the down linemen to fire low at the thighs in order to chop the defensive linemen down on Quick Passes.

COMBO

Combo is a block between two offensive linemen—or one tackle and one tight end—that doubles a defensive lineman back to a linebacker. As they are driving this defender between their triangle, they place their eyes on the linebacker working towards the hole. They should think, "Hands on, eyes on." This means hands on the down lineman, but eyes on the linebacker. If the backer tries to break to either side, the down lineman (or tight end) to that side comes off to seal block. Figures 5-14 and 5-15 illustrate two examples of combo blocks.

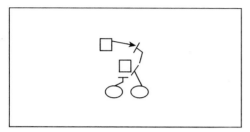

Figure 5-14. Combo—Variation A

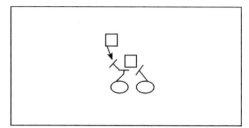

Figure 5-15. Combo—Variation B

COUNTER

Counter is a blocking scheme where the playside center, guard, tackle, and tight end block down, so the backside guard and tackle can pull. The down blocks must take care of the defensive tackles and noseguards with double-team blocks on the playside and combos on the backside. Figures 5-16 through 5-18 illustrate examples of 26, 46, and 66 Counter. The backside guard OG blocks as the backside tackle leads into the hole.

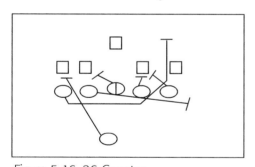

Figure 5-16. 26 Counter

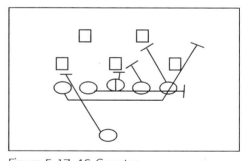

Figure 5-17. 46 Counter

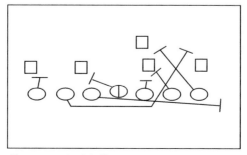

Figure 5-18. 66 Counter

CUT

Cut is a block used in the open field in which the offensive man runs up to the defender and breaks down at the last possible second to place his inside shoulder on the defender's outside thigh. This block is used by the fullback on toss, the tight end on a veer-release block, offensive linemen on screens, pulling linemen on GOGs, and receivers on open-field blocks.

DOUBLE

In a double block, two offensive players combine to block one defender. This block is similar to a combo block, except the two offensive players try to drive their defender so far back that it cuts off the linebacker's pursuit. On a double-team, the defender should be totally blocked out of the play. The outside offensive lineman (or tight end) places the triangle on the outside number of the defender. The inside offensive lineman places the triangle on the inside number. If done correctly, the defender should cut off the linebacker as he is placed on his back (Figures 5-19 and 5-20).

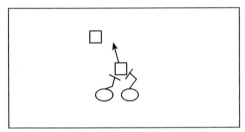

Figure 5-19. Double block—Variation A

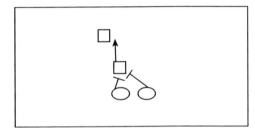

Figure 5-20. Double block—Variation B

DOWN

Down tells an offensive lineman to step with his inside foot directly in front of the covered offensive lineman on his inside. If the inside lineman is uncovered, the down block steps toward the linebacker at a 45 degree angle. The down block's contact point for an offensive lineman is the inside V of his neck. If the down-blocking offensive lineman is covered, he may have to rip through the inside shoulder of the defensive lineman to down block a linebacker. Figures 5-21 through 5-23 illustrate down blocks used on traps.

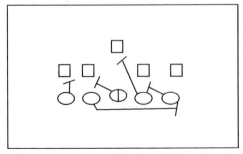

Figure 5-21. Down block—Variation A

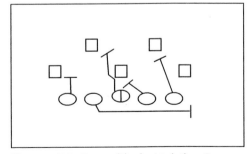

Figure 5-22. Down block—Variation B

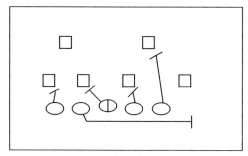

Figure 5-23. Down block—Variation C

DRAW

Draw tells the offensive lineman to invite the defensive lineman to run outside the running lane of the draw's location. The offensive lineman must know where the draw is going before taking a 12-inch drop step. The hinge step invites the defensive lineman to run up field. As the defensive lineman rushes, the offensive lineman pushes that defender past the running lane. The uncovered offensive lineman takes a drop step, then attacks the linebacker. The center and guards can always use an X block with this same draw technique. The draw can also use a lead block from a back on a linebacker. Figures 5-24 through 5-26 illustrate 22 Draw, 42 Lead Draw, and 23 X Draw.

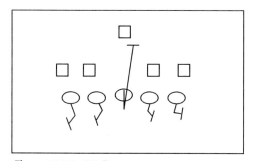

Figure 5-24. 22 Draw

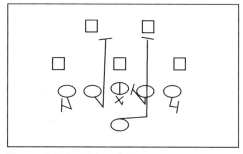

Figure 5-25. 42 Lead Draw

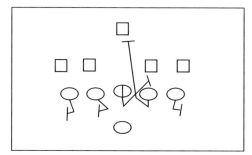

Figure 5-26. 23 X Draw

FAN

Fan is a Big on Big pass protection where the offensive linemen take two toe-heel drop steps. The objective is to form area pass protection. The offensive linemen stay at home if the defensive linemen cross. This is a seven-step drop. The line should extend their arms and force the defenders outside if possible. Uncovered linemen help pass protect (Figures 5-27 through 5-29).

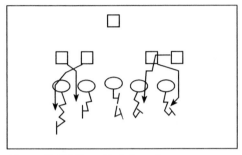

Figure 5-27. Fan—Variation A

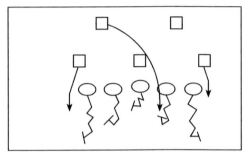

Figure 5-28. Fan—Variation B

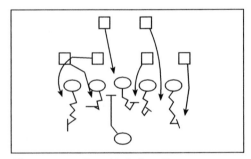

Figure 5-29. Fan—Variation C

G

G tells the playside guard to kick-out or roll block the last man on the line of scrimmage. The playside guard wants to block the defensive end in the direction he is going. If the defensive end steps forward and up, the guard blocks with the outside V of his neck on the defensive end's inside hip. If the defensive end comes flat inside behind the tackle's or tight end's down block, the guard rolls him inside by using the inside V of his neck on the outside hip. If the defensive end squats in the hole, the guard can cut block. Figures 5-30 through 5-32 illustrate three examples of G.

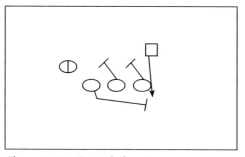

Figure 5-30. G—Variation A

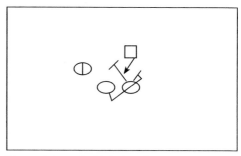

Figure 5-31. G—Variation B

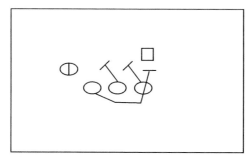

Figure 5-32. G—Variation C

GT

GT tells the playside guard and tackle to pull. Even if both linemen are covered, they pull laterally to the outside to chop block secondary defenders. The center will zone block playside (Figure 5-33).

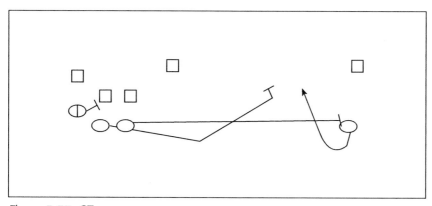

Figure 5-33. GT

GOG

GOG tells both guards to pull playside. If the playside guard and tackle are both covered, the playside guard must stay, unless the uncovered center is going to reach the playside defensive tackle. The playside tight end hook blocks, and the uncovered center down blocks. If the playside tackle is covered, he hook blocks. If the playside tackle is uncovered, he down blocks. The playside guard blocks the force man and the backside guard seals pursuit. Figures 5-34 through 5-36 illustrate examples of 28 GOG, 48 GOG, and 68 GOG.

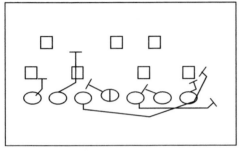

Figure 5-34. 28 GOG

Figure 5-35. 48 GOG

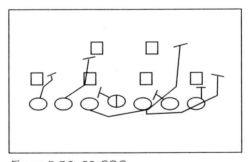

Figure 5-36. 68 GOG

HOOK

Hook tells an offensive lineman to shuffle step with his playside foot at a 90-degree angle and place his head on the outside shoulder of the defender as he moves his butt to the side of the hole. The hook block is very important for all the toss plays. Figures 5-37 and 5-38 illustrate hook blocks by the tight end and playside tackle on 48 Toss.

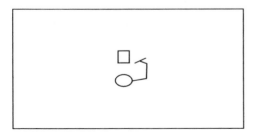

Figure 5-37. Tight end hook block—48 Toss

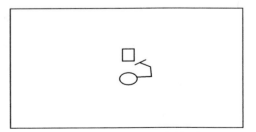

Figure 5-38. Playside tackle hook block—48 Toss

IN

In is a combo block by the playside tackle and guard. In the flanker formation, the playside uncovered tackle can release up to the playside linebacker if the guard has a 2i technique. The playside tight end will veer release and cut block the force man unless the block is called *In Seal*. *Seal* tells the tight end to come inside and block the defender aligned over the playside tackle. If necessary, this also allows the tackle to combo block inside. If the playside guard is uncovered, he can also combo block with the center, or release up to linebackers. Figures 5-39 through 5-43 illustrate several examples of 14 In.

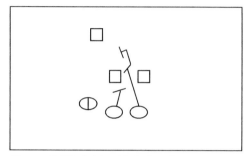

Figure 5-39. 14 In—Variation A

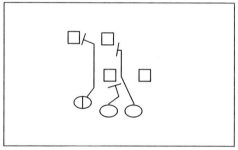

Figure 5-40. 14 In—Variation B

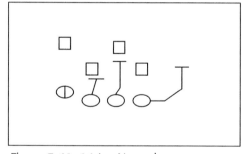

Figure 5-41. 14 In—Normal

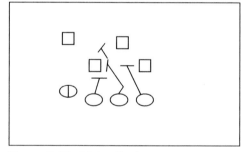

Figure 5-42. 14 In—Seal

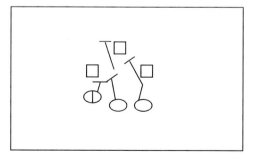

Figure 5-43. 14 In—Variation C

LEAD

Lead is a double-team block at the point of attack and a climb block by the lead back. The uncovered lineman will double-team the closest down lineman at the point of attack. The only exception is when the Lead is called between two 3 techniques with two stacked middle linebackers. The center will have the playside backer while the fullback climb blocks the backside middle backer. This running play can be called at any location between the tackles. Figures 5-44 through 5-46 illustrate 40, 42, and 64 Lead blocking.

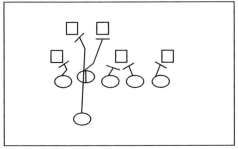

Figure 5-44. 40 Lead

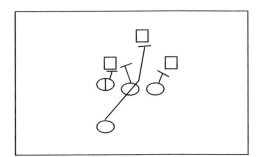

Figure 5-45. 42 Lead

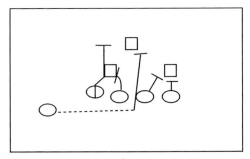

Figure 5-46. 64 Lead

LOAD

Load is a block by the fullback or motion back that is made on the playside defensive end. The load block is used on 16 and 17 Load, and on power running plays. The objective is to kick the defensive end outside or roll block him inside. If the defensive end steps up, the back will cut the defensive end with his outside shoulder on the defensive end's inside thigh. If the defensive end slides down inside, the back will use his inside shoulder on the outside thigh. If the defensive end squats in the hole, the back can cut with either shoulder.

MIDLINE

Midline tells the playside guard to release inside and double-team, or combo block with the center. The playside tackle out blocks any defender outside, so the motion back can lead on the playside linebacker. Figures 5-47 through 5-49 illustrate three Midline blocks.

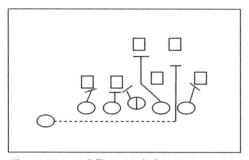

Figure 5-47. Midline—Variation A

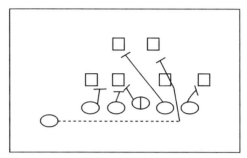

Figure 5-48. Midline—Variation B

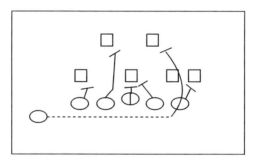

Figure 5-49. Midline—Variation C

CHOP

Chop tells the offensive lineman to fire out low and hit the defensive lineman in the thighs. The offensive lineman comes off the ball with his head up, but quickly drops down for the chop block.

OG

OG tells the backside guard to pull playside around the end to block the force man, or kick-out the first defender head-up or outside the end. The backside guard can roll, cut, or kick-out block this defender. If uncovered, the center must block down on the backside guard's defender. Figures 5-50 through 5-52 illustrate 14 OG Left, 27 Bootleg Right, and 15 OG Right.

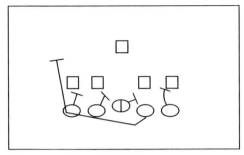
Figure 5-50. 14 OG Left

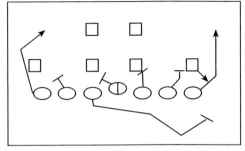
Figure 5-51. 27 Bootleg Right

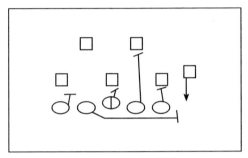
Figure 5-52. 15 OG Right

OUT

Out tells the offensive lineman to place the triangle on the defender's inside number and turn his butt inside towards the hole. The lineman steps first with his near foot to gain position. The angle he steps in depends on the position of the defender. Out can also be the Outside Veer, which is like zone blocking, except the playside tight end down blocks.

POWER

Power tells the fullback or motion back to load block the last man on the line of scrimmage. Power also tells the backside guard to OG pull and lead up into the hole on linebackers or secondary. The playside tight end, tackle, guard, and center down and combo block. The three offensive linemen and tight end create a wall by stepping down inside at a 45 degree angle. They attempt to place defenders on the V of their inside neck. Figures 5-53 through 5-55 illustrate 46 Power, 47 Power, and 66 Power.

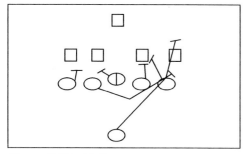

Figure 5-53. 46 Power

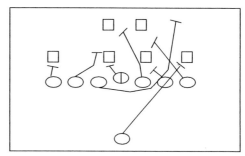

Figure 5-54. 47 Power

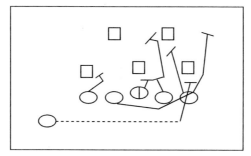

Figure 5-55. 66 Power

QUICK

Quick tells the offensive linemen to aggressively pass protect. On slant routes, linemen can also chop block their defenders.

ROLL

Roll tells a pulling guard or back to seal a defender who has come hard inside behind a down block. The blocker rolls the defender's shoulders to the inside. The block is made with the inside V of the neck on the defender's outside number. You can also use the triangle on the outside number.

SPEED

Speed tells the playside tackle to release directly upfield to seal or hook block a defender in front and on his inside. The playside tackle releases the last man on the line of scrimmage if he aligns outside his numbers. If you're facing two defenders outside an open-end tackle, the tackle must block the 4/5 technique. If the playside tackle is in the flanker formation, he zone blocks. The playside tight end combo blocks with the playside tackle. The rest of the offensive line zone blocks playside. Figures 5-56 through 5-58 illustrate three examples of 18 Speed.

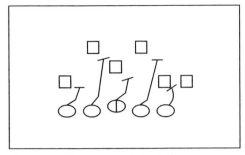
Figure 5-56. 18 Speed—Variation A

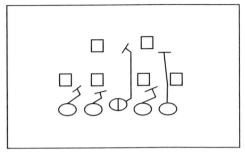
Figure 5-57. 18 Speed—Variation B

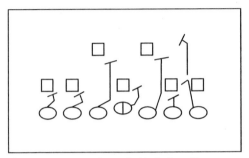
Figure 5-58. 18 Speed—Variation C

STALK

Stalk tells the receiver to mirror the defender and to stay between him and the runner. The release should be at the inside V of the defender's neck. If the defender is in a tight-man coverage, the receiver may want to first try to run the defender off by getting him to turn his shoulders away from the ball. The receiver should watch the defender's eyes for his direction. If the defender comes hard, the receiver/back can also cut him.

STOP

Stop is a Big on Big pass protection in which the offensive linemen take only one heel-toe step as they bring the weight over their feet. The offensive linemen should quickly bring their hands into the armpits of the defensive lineman. They should not lunge or reach for the defender, and should allow the defender to engage, but should stop his penetration by lifting through the armpits.

TRAP

Trap tells the backside guard to kick-out the first down lineman head-up or outside the playside guard. The playside guard makes a call by yelling, "You," or, "Me." This signal/call tells the playside tackle and guard their assignments. "You" tells the playside tackle to down block the playside linebacker because the playside guard is going to combo, release inside with the center, or influence behind the playside tackle. "Me" tells the playside tackle to base block because the playside guard is going to block the playside linebacker. The playside guard always calls "You" if he cannot release up to the middle backer, but first the playside guard must always block down on any defender who is in the A gap or covering the center. Figures 5-59 through 5-64 illustrate several examples of 20 Trap calls.

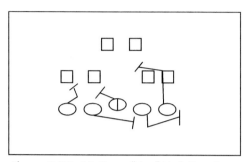

Figure 5-59. 20 Trap—"You" Variation A

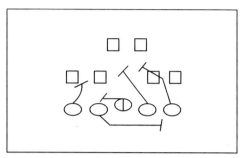

Figure 5-60. 20 Trap—"You" Variation B

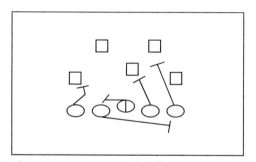

Figure 5-61. 20 Trap—"You" Variation C

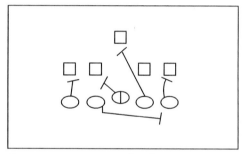

Figure 5-62. 20 Trap—"Me"

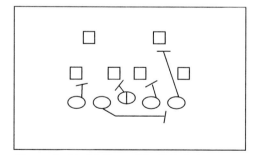

Figure 5-63. 20 Trap—"You" Variation D

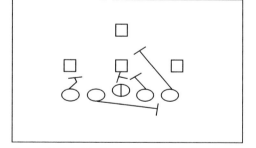

Figure 5-64. 20 Trap—"You" Variation E

TRIANGLE

Triangle is a blocking technique in which the offensive lineman makes a triangle with both hands, with his face mask between. The triangle can be in the middle or on either number.

UNDER

Under tells the playside tight end to fold under the tackle's out block on his defender. The playside tight end then cut blocks the playside linebacker. This call is usually made on midline option with no motion (Figures 5-65 and 5-66).

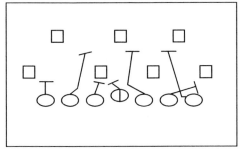

Figure 5-65. 10 Midline—Variation A

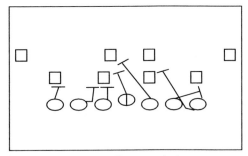

Figure 5-66. 10 Midline—Variation B

X

X tells the backside guard and center to exchange base blocks. First, the uncovered lineman blocks down as the covered lineman steps behind and up for the linebacker. Figures 5-67 through 5-69 illustrate 14 X and 22 X.

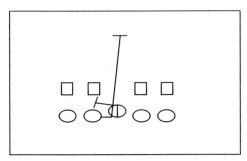

Figure 5-67. 14 X—Variation A

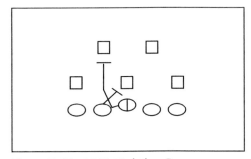

Figure 5-68. 14 X—Variation B

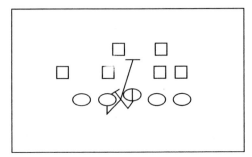

Figure 5-69. 22 X

ZONE

Zone tells the entire offensive line and tight ends to take a lateral step at a 90-degree angle with their playside foot. Then, as their second and third backside steps land, they begin to turn up field to lock on to the defender. If the offensive lineman or tight end is covered, he will most likely block this defender as long as the defensive lineman does not slant in the opposite direction.

If a zone blocker is uncovered, he steps laterally at a 90-degree angle to stop any outside slants. If no slant occurs, the zone-stepping lineman tries to reach the *Next Man Over*. Next man over tells the lineman to reach his helmet across the next defender. The exception is the last man on the line of scrimmage. He does not release his defender until the inside lineman next to him takes over the block.

If the defender is any good, he will read the offensive down lineman's helmet and step laterally with the zoning lineman. So most of the time, the linemen will still block the same individuals. Figures 5-70 through 5-72 illustrate 28, 48, and 68 Toss.

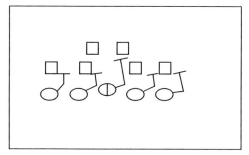

Figure 5-70. 28 Toss

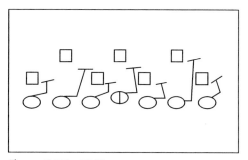

Figure 5-71. 48 Toss

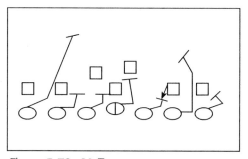

Figure 5-72. 68 Toss

CHAPTER 6

Option Series

The inside veer (14 and 15 In) is the base play of the spread option offense. Other options include the midline option (10 and 11 Mid), the outside veer (16 and 17 Out), and the speed option (18 and 19 Speed).

The inside veer, outside veer, and speed option each have variations. When giving straight to the fullback off the veer action, say the word *base* (12 and 13 Base). On the inside veer, veer release the tight end or back to block the force man while the playside tackle blocks down. You can also change the blocking scheme with the tight end blocking down and sealing on the linebacker (14 and 15 In Seal) versus a 4-3 defense. To have the playside slot or flanker block inside on the linebacker, use the word *Crack*. These plays can use short or medium motion when a back is the pitchman.

The inside veer can use a G block (14G and 15G), which tells the quarterback to fake to the fullback and then follow the guard around or under the defensive end. Another way to have the quarterback keep is to call a load block off the outside veer action (16 Load or 17 Load), which tells the fullback to cut the last man on the line of scrimmage. To give the ball to the fullback off-tackle, call a G block (16G and 17G).

The spread option offense has two types of misdirection plays off the inside veer: 14/15 X and 14/15 OG. The X block tells the backside guard and the center to exchange blocking assignments. The OG block tells the guard on the side of the fullback's fake to pull opposite and lead for the quarterback.

The speed option uses one back. It can attack the strong, weak, or balanced side (18 Speed and 19 Speed). Speed option is designed to release the last man on the line of scrimmage, so the quarterback can pitch to the one back. If you want the quarterback to keep the ball, call for a zone block (18 Zone and 19 Zone). This usually turns into a cutback for the quarterback.

The Midline Option is designed to use medium or no motion (10 Mid and 11 Mid). The playside tackle blocks out as the playside guard releases inside on a linebacker or a double-team. This releases the defensive tackle for the quarterback to read.

SPREAD OPTION OFFENSE PLAYBOOK

Play List:	14 and 15 OG
10 and 11 Midline	16 and 17 Out
12 and 13 Base	16 and 17 G
14 and 15 In	16 and 17 Load
14 and 15 X	18 and 19 Speed
14 and 15 G	18 and 19 Zone
14 and 15 Belly G	

Abbreviations List:	Q – Quarterback
PT – Playside Tackle	B – Back
BT – Backside Tackle	F – Fullback
PG – Playside Guard	MB – Motion Back
BG – Backside Guard	PTE – Playside Tight End
C – Center	BTE – Backside Tight End
	SE – Split End

Rules for 10 and 11 Midline:

PT – Out blocks second down lineman from C.

BT – Base blocks.

PG – Down blocks first inside defender.

BG – Base blocks.

C – Down blocks if uncovered or base blocks if covered.

PTE – Cut blocks force or under block if called.

BTE – Base blocks.

SE – Stalk blocks.

MB – In medium motion, cuts inside PT and PG for lead block on playside LB. In short motion, acts as the pitchman.

B – Stalk blocks.

F – Dives directly at Q's butt for a possible give.

Q – Reads first defender over and outside PG's position. Runs playside B/C gap on keep. Medium motion does not have a pitchman. Short motion has a pitchman with an under PTE block.

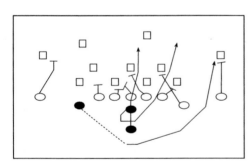

Figure 6-1. Lip 11—Variation A

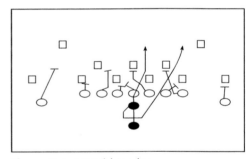

Figure 6-2. Lip 11—Variation B

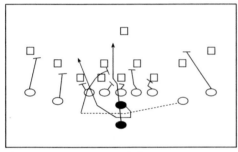

Figure 6-3. Roy 10 Mid

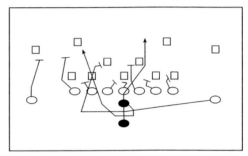

Figure 6-4. 10 Mid Under

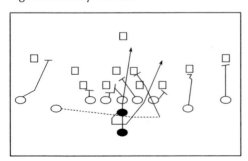

Figure 6-5. Rip 10 Mid

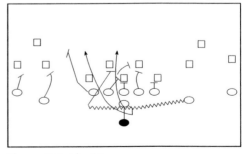

Figure 6-6. Lip 11

Rules for 12 and 13 Base:

Line – Base block. (PT/base P2, BT/base B2, PG/base P1, BG/base B1, C/base 0)

TEs – Base block P3.

SE – Stalk block.

MB - Short or medium motion and acts as pitchman to draw linebackers.

B – Stalk block.

F – Dives at inside hip of PG and cuts off PG's base block after automatic give.

Q – Checks A and B gap. Opens playside for automatic give. Continues on option.

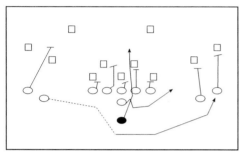

Figure 6-7. Roy 12 Base

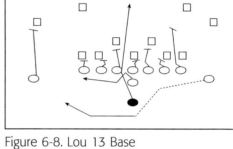

Figure 6-8. Lou 13 Base

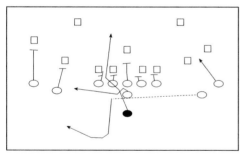

Figure 6-9. Lip 13 Base

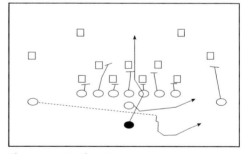

Figure 6-10. Rip 12 Base

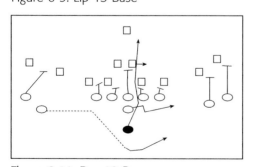

Figure 6-11. Roy 12 Base

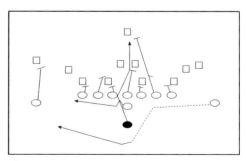

Figure 6-12. Lou 13 Base

Rules for 14 and 15 In:

PT – Combo blocks inside with PG.

BT – Zone blocks.

PG – If uncovered, checks inside for combo block. If covered, PG calls for combo block from PT or base blocks.

BG – Zone blocks.

C – Calls for a combo block from PG if defender is in playside A gap.

PTE – Veer or seal blocks.

BTE – Zone blocks.

SE – Stalk blocks.

MB – Becomes pitchman.

B – Stalk blocks or crack-back block.

F – Dives directly at the PG's outside hip for a possible give. If ball is pushed into F's stomach, it is F's ball. If ball is placed on F's hip, Q will keep. F cuts defenders with strong fake.

Q – Reads the first down lineman over or outside the PT. If this defender steps up field or squats, Q gives to F by pushing the ball into the stomach. Q cannot pull the ball once he has pushed it into F's stomach. If the down lineman slants inside for F's dive, Q puts ball on the hip, keeps, and runs downhill off-tackle until next defender forces him to pitch. If the defense has two down linemen head-up and outside the PT, Q pitches quickly, or changes the play.

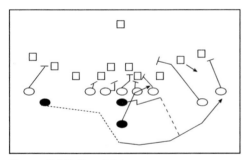

Figure 6-13. Roy 14 In

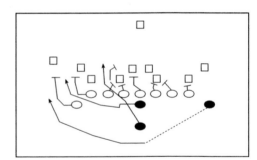

Figure 6-14. Roy 15 In

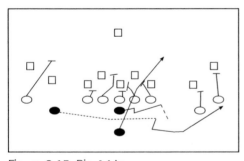

Figure 6-15. Rip 14 In

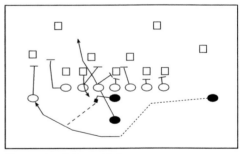

Figure 6-16. Lou 15 In

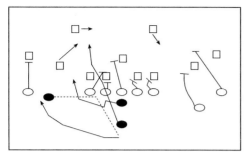

Figure 6-17. Roy 15 In

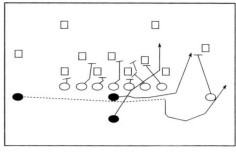

Figure 6-18. Rip 14 In Seal

Rules for 14 and 15 X:

PT – Base blocks.

BT – Base blocks defender outside.

PG – Base blocks.

BG – X blocks with C.

C – X blocks with BG.

TEs – Base block.

SE – Stalk blocks.

MB – Acts as a pitchman, but in the opposite direction.

B – Base blocks.

F – Dives at the hole called for a fake handoff.

Q – Fakes to FB over the hole called, but turns back inside to run behind the X block.

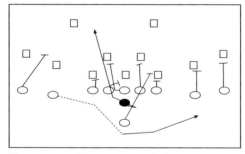

Figure 6-19. Roy 14 X–Variation A

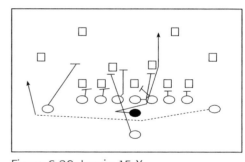

Figure 6-20. Lassie 15 X

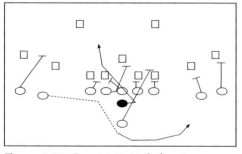

Figure 6-21. Roy 14 X–Variation B

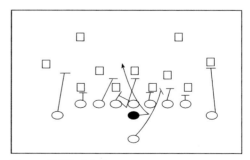

Figure 6-22. 14 X

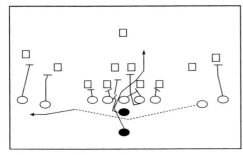

Figure 6-23. Larry 15 X

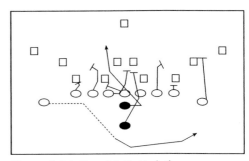

Figure 6-24. Roy 14 X—Variation

Rules for 14 and 15 G:

PT – Hook blocks if PG is uncovered, or blocks down if PG is covered. On Belly G, TE will hook block.

BT – Zone blocks.

PG – G blocks last man on the line of scrimmage. On Belly G, PG comes around PT and turns up the field at first opportunity to block force.

BG – Zone blocks.

C – Zone blocks playside.

PTE – Combo blocks first defender inside. On Belly G, PTE hook blocks.

BTE – Zone blocks.

SE – Stalk blocks.

MB – Becomes the pitchman.

B – Stalk blocks or crack-back blocks.

F – Dives directly at the pulling PG as he makes his fake to cut off the playside LB. Hits any defender directly in front. On Belly G, F takes two steps towards hole, but then belly's around the end to block playside LB.

Q – Fakes into the stomach of F. Pulls and follows PG. PG may kick-out or log block, so Q must read PG's block. Q attacks downhill until made to pitch. On Belly, Q reverses out.

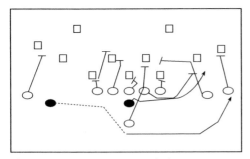

Figure 6-25. Roy 14 G—Variation A

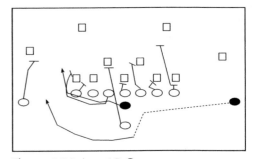

Figure 6-26. Lou 15 G

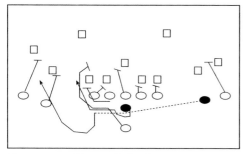

Figure 6-27. Lip 15 Belly G

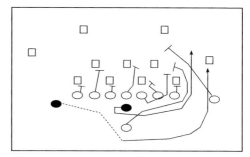

Figure 6-28. Roy 14 Belly G

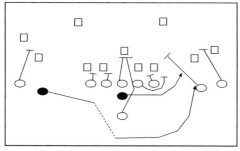

Figure 6-29. Roy 14 G—Variation B

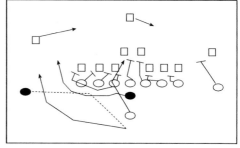

Figure 6-30. Roy 15 G

Rules for 14 and 15 OG:

PT – Hook blocks. If call is Down OG, PT combo blocks inside.

BT – Base blocks.

PG – Hook blocks.

BG – OG blocks first defender in front or outside the PT.

C – Blocks down on BG's defender if uncovered. Base blocks if covered.

PTE – Hook blocks.

BTE – Base blocks.

SE – Stalk blocks.

F – Dives at hole called to fill for the pulling BG.

MB – Uses short motion and breaks opposite the hole called to be pitchman.

B – Stalk blocks.

Q – Fakes towards hole called, but turns back inside to follow the BG around or under the PTE. Q can pitch if he gets pressure. Q may cut underneath the BG's OG block.

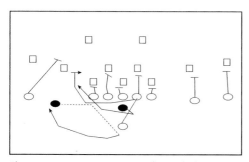

Figure 6-31. Roy 14 OG Left—Variation A

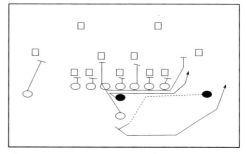

Figure 6-32. Lou 15 OG Right

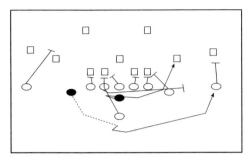

Figure 6-33. Roy 15 OG Right—Variation A

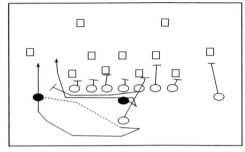

Figure 6-34. Roy 14 OG Left—Variation B

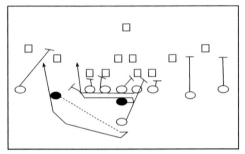

Figure 6-35. Roy 14 OG Left—Variation C

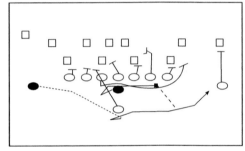

Figure 6-36. Roy 15 OG Right—Variation B

Rules for 16 and 17 Out:

PT – Zone blocks. PT can call for a combo block from PTE.

BTE/BT/BG/C/PG – Zone block playside.

PTE – Blocks down to combo block with PT.

SE – Stalk blocks.

MB – Becomes the pitchman.

B – Stalk blocks.

F – Takes a lateral slide step towards the outside hip of the PT. Q will put the ball into F's stomach and ride him towards the hole for two steps. Q can leave or pull the ball. If Q pulls the ball, F continues off-tackle. If Q pushes the ball hard into the stomach as he slides his back hand out, the ball is given to F.

Q – Opens playside and reaches the ball deep towards F. Q wants to take at least two lateral steps towards the hole with the ball in F's stomach. During this time, Q reads the first defender outside the PT. If this defender (last man on the line of scrimmage) comes down inside, Q pulls the ball and attacks the next level. If the defender steps up, around, or sits, Q slides his bottom hand out as he pushes the ball into F's stomach.

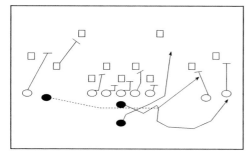

Figure 6-37. Rip 16 Out

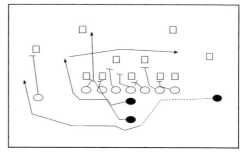

Figure 6-38. Lou 17 Out—Variation A

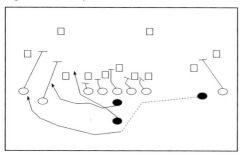

Figure 6-39. Lou 17 Out—Variation B

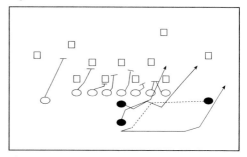

Figure 6-40. Lou 16 Out

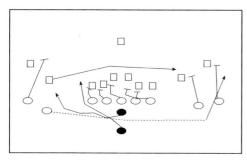

Figure 6-41. Reggie 17 Out

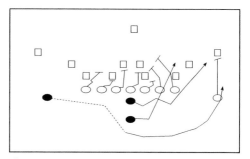

Figure 6-42. Roy 16 Out

Rules for 16 and 17 G:

PT – Hook blocks if PG is uncovered, or blocks down if PG is covered.

BT – Zone blocks.

PG – G blocks last man on the line of scrimmage. PG can kick-out or roll block his G block.

BG – Zone blocks.

C – Zone blocks playside.

PTE – Combo blocks to first defender inside.

BTE – Zone blocks.

SE – Stalk blocks.

MB – Becomes the pitchman.

B – Stalk blocks or crack-back blocks.

F – Takes a lateral step and then comes downhill towards the outside hip of PT for the automatic handoff. F usually cuts underneath the PG's G block.

Q – Opens playside with option action. Q gives the ball to F and then continues with option action.

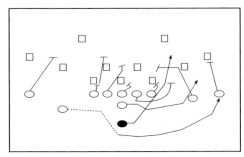

Figure 6-43. Roy 16 G—Variation A

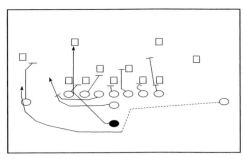

Figure 6-44. Lou 17 G

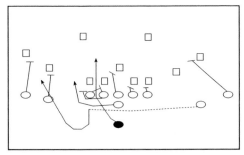

Figure 6-45. Lip 17 G—Variation A

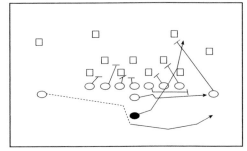

Figure 6-46. Roy 16 G—Variation B

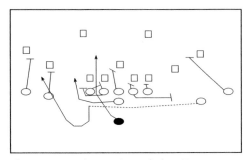

Figure 6-47. Lip 17 G—Variation B

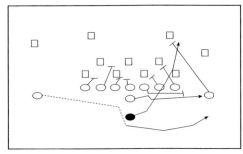

Figure 6-48. Roy 16 G

Rules for 16 and 17 Load:

Offensive Line – Zone blocks playside.

PTE – Veer releases and blocks force.

BTE – Zone blocks.

SE – Stalk blocks.

MB – Becomes the pitchman.

B – Releases defender and goes to safety, unless a crack-back block is called on the playside linebacker.

F – Goes directly to cut block the P3 defender/first defender outside PT. In slot/twins, this defender could be a 9 technique or outside linebacker. In the flanker formation, the defender will usually be in front of the PTE.

Q – Releases hard laterally around the last man on the line of scrimmage. Keeps until he is forced to pitch.

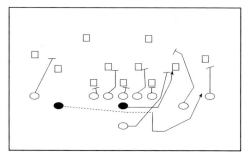

Figure 6-49. Rip 16 Load

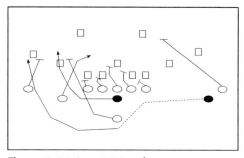

Figure 6-50. Lou 16 Load

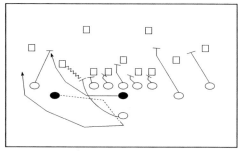

Figure 6-51. Roy 17 Load

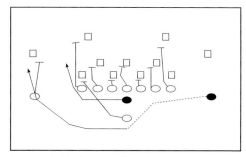

Figure 6-52. Lou 17 Load

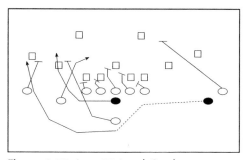

Figure 6-53. Lou 17 Load Crack

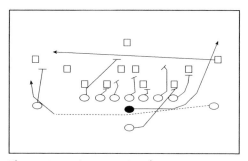

Figure 6-54. Larry 16 Load

Rules for 18 and 19 Speed:

PT – Releases the last man on the line of scrimmage in slot/twins. In flanker/wing, PT zone blocks playside. If the play is 18/19 Zone, PT zone blocks in slot/twins.

BT/PG/C/BG/BT/BY – Zone block.

PTE – Veer releases to force man. If play is called 18/19 Zone, then the PTE zone blocks.

MB – Stalk blocks first defender that shows.

B – Stalk blocks or crack-back blocks if called.

F – Becomes the pitchman.

Q – Takes a back step and then attacks the inside leg of the last man on the line of scrimmage. When defender steps up or squats, Q pitches to F. If defender flies out towards F, Q keeps and runs downhill. If the play is 18/19 Zone, Q releases laterally around the last man on the line of scrimmage and keeps until made to pitch. Q can also cut back on the line of scrimmage if he has an opening.

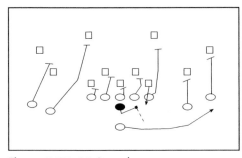

Figure 6-55. 18 Speed

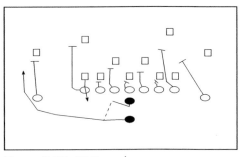

Figure 6-56. 19 Speed

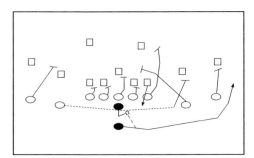

Figure 6-57. Rip 18 Speed Crack

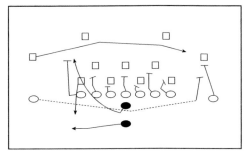

Figure 6-58. Reggie 19 Speed—Variation A

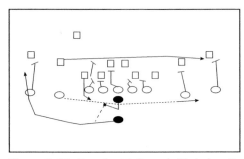

Figure 6-59. Reggie 19 Speed—Variation B

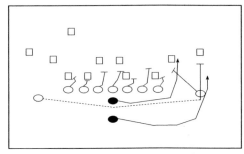

Figure 6-60. Reggie 18 Zone Crack

OPTION PLAYS FROM THE WING FORMATION

The wing formation also uses the option series. If a team wants to get outside, they can bring the defense in tight with the wing formation. Figures 6-61 through 6-68 illustrate most of the option plays out of the wing formation.

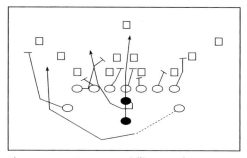

Figure 6-61. Lou 11 Midline Under

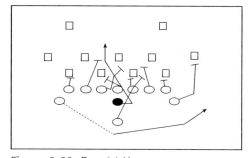

Figure 6-62. Roy 14 X

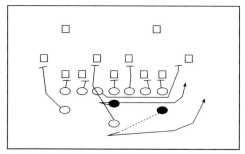

Figure 6-63. Lou 15 OG Right

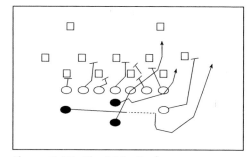

Figure 6-64. Rip 14 In Seal

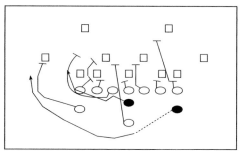

Figure 6-65. Lou 15 G

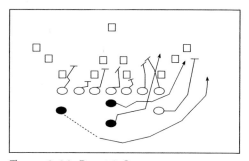

Figure 6-66. Roy 16 Out

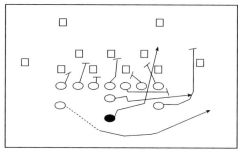

Figure 6-67. Roy 16 G

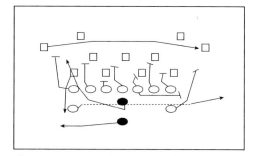

Figure 6-68. Reggie 19 Speed

CHAPTER 7

Power Series

When you are evenly matched up with your opponent, or the weather is not conducive for the option/passing game, a conservative running attack can be a positive addition. The Power Series uses trap, lead, bounce, counter, power, GOG, and zone blocks. You can run these plays from any formation in the 20, 40, and 60 Series

20 AND 21 TRAP

20 and 21 Trap are gives to the fullback over the center. Before the cadence, the playside guard makes a *You* or *Me* line call to direct the playside tackle and guard (Figures 7-1 through 7-4).

Rules for 20 and 21 Trap:

PT – Comes hard inside to playside linebacker on *You* call. The playside tackle base blocks on *Me* call.

PG – Makes the line call on the line of scrimmage. If the playside guard calls *Me*, he comes hard inside to playside middle backer because the center is uncovered and the playside guard has a direct line to the middle backer. On all other calls, the playside guard calls *You*. *You* tells the PT to go inside to down block on playside linebacker. PG's first rule is to block down or combo any defender in the A gap between him and the center. PG also combo blocks when center is covered. The playside guard also blocks back on the second middle backer versus the split. If the center is uncovered, but PG has a 2 technique, PG makes a *You* call, so he can influence and block the defender over the PT.

C – Can make a front call. Uncovered, the center blocks back for the trapping backside guard. Covered, the center doubles with the playside guard.

BG – Trap blocks first defender head-up and past the center.

PTE/BTE – Base block.

SE/B – Base/stalk block.

MB – In short motion fakes a handoff from the quarterback. M can also stalk block if in lateral motion.

F – Dives at the back of the quarterback and then cuts back as soon as he gets the handoff. F makes a second cut after going underneath the guard.

Q – Opens opposite the side of the hole called, but steps back as he takes the snap, so the backside guard can come between him and the center. The quarterback then gives to the fullback and shows option to the backside. If the motion back is in short motion, the quarterback can fake to him as he bootlegs.

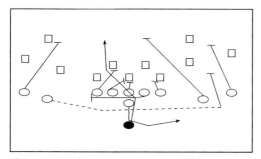

Figure 7-1. Slot Reggie—21 Trap Left

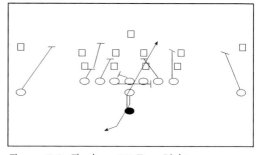

Figure 7-2. Flanker—20 Trap Right

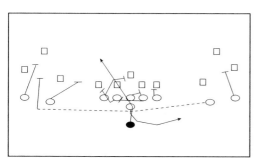

Figure 7-3. Slot Larry—21 Trap Left

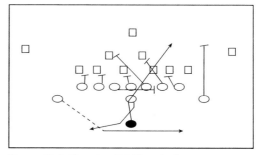

Figure 7-4. Reggie—21 Trap Left

22 AND 23 DRAW

22 and 23 Draw are fullback draws off the dropback action. These draws can use an X Block to the playside or backside. If 62 or 63 is called, the fullback and tailback switch (Figures 7-5 and 7-6).

Rules for 22 and 23 Draw:

Line – Raise up and hinge as if to pass block and then block their defender away from the hole. The playside guard and center can execute the X block. The uncovered lineman down blocks on the covered lineman. The covered lineman then comes around for the linebacker.

SE/B – Run defenders off and then stalk block.

TEs – run defenders off.

MB – Goes in long or extra-long motion to run off, or stalk blocks.

F – Raises up and steps to the side called. The fullback waits for the ball and then runs towards the X block, and looks for daylight.

Q – Opens to the side called and gives the ball to the fullback. The quarterback then continues away in the same direction.

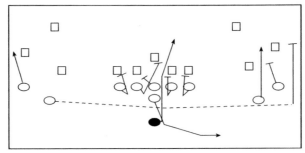

Figure 7-5. Slot Rover—22 Draw X Left

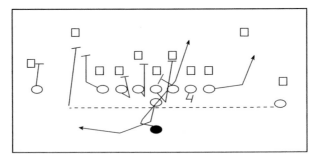

Figure 7-6. Flanker Larry—63 Draw X Right

26 AND 27 COUNTER

26 and 27 Counter are fullback off-tackle plays that pull the backside guard and tackle to the playside. Calling 66 or 67 Counter tells the fullback and tailback to switch positions (Figures 7-7 and 7-8).

Rules for 26 and 27 Counter:

PT/PG/C – All down block to the inside.

BG – Pulls playside to kick-out or roll block the last defender on the line of scrimmage.

BT – Follows the backside guard and reads his block. If the backside guard kicks out the last defender on the line of scrimmage, the backside tackle cuts underneath and lead blocks for the back. If the backside guard roll blocks his defender, the backside tackle comes around and still leads for the back.

TEs – Both playside and backside always block down inside to C gap.

B/SE/MB – Base/stalk block. On 66 and 67 Counter, the tailback and fullback switch positions.

F – Takes a hop step away from the hole as if he is going to receive a pitch, but then returns hard downhill for a handoff from the quarterback. The fullback follows the backside tackle into the hole.

Q – Opens 45 degrees away and slightly back from the hole, but then breaks back and hands off to the fullback. The quarterback then bootlegs to the side he opened on the snap.

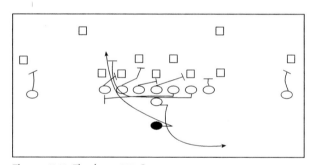

Figure 7-7. Flanker–27 Counter

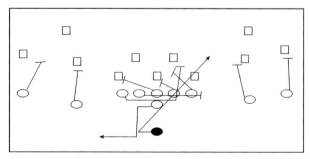

Figure 7-8. Slot–26 Counter

95

28 AND 29 ZONE

28 and 29 Zone are pitches to the fullback with zone blocking. 68 and 69 Toss tells the fullback and tailback to switch positions (Figures 7-9 and 7-10).

Rules for 28 and 29 Zone:

Line/TE – Zone block to the side called. They must stay in contact with their defender.

SE/B – Stalk/base block.

MB – Goes in medium motion and blocks first threat.

F – Releases hard laterally for the pitch by stepping first with his playside foot at a 90-degree angle. The fullback can get to the outside or cut back.

Q – Reverses out and pitches to the fullback. The quarterback continues in the same direction to provide additional protection.

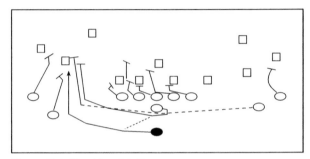

Figure 7-9 Slot Lip—29 Zone

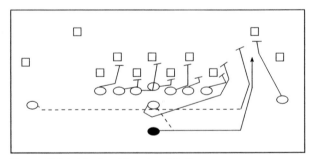

Figure 7-10. Flanker Reggie—68 Zone

LEAD CHECK-WITH-ME

Lead Check-With-Me is a two-back isolation play where the hole is called on the line of scrimmage. The second number called in the sequence is the actual play. The check-with-me can also be called using medium motion in the sixty series (Figures 7-11 and 7–12).

Rules for Lead Check-With-Me:

Line – Waits for the quarterback to call the hole on the line of scrimmage. The quarterback will call a hole that is not covered by a lineman. The lineman over that hole will be uncovered. The uncovered lineman blocks the closest down lineman to the right or left. The rest of the linemen base block their defenders away from the hole.

TEs – Out block their defenders away from the hole.

B – Base blocks. On 66 and 67 Power the tailback and fullback switch.

MB – Goes into short motion behind the fullback and listens for the hole called by the quarterback.

F – Listens for the hole called and lead blocks the linebacker over the hole.

Q – Checks the offensive line for an uncovered offensive lineman. He then calls the hole (40, 41, 42, 43, 44, or 45) of the uncovered area to direct the fullback and motion back at that hole. The quarterback reverses out to hand the ball to the motion back. He then shows pass.

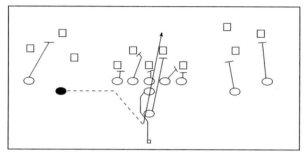

Figure 7-11. Slot Roy—Lead Check-With-Me—"31-42, 31-42"

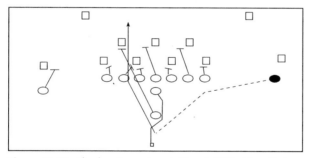

Figure 7-12. Flanker Lou—Lead Check-With-Me—"14-45, 14-45"

BOUNCE

Bounce is an outside two-back play that first appears to be a lead run. Bounce is called 44 and 45 Bounce to the motion man in short motion, or 64 and 65 Bounce to the tailback with medium motion (Figures 7-13 and 7-14).

Rules for Bounce:

PT – Takes one inside base step and then hook blocks his defender. (You want the defense to think inside.)

BT – Zone blocks playside.

PG – Takes one inside base step and then hook blocks his defender.

C – Zone blocks playside.

PTE – Takes one short inside base step and then hook blocks.

BTE – Zone blocks playside.

MB – On medium motion (64 and 65 Bounce), takes two steps downhill as if to block for the lead, but then plants with inside leg to go outside around the end for the seal block. On short motion (44 and 45 Bounce), MB comes downhill towards the hole called, but cuts outside and follows the lead blocker.

F – Takes two hard steps towards the playside linebacker, then bounces around the tight end to seal block.

T – On 64 and 65 Bounce, comes downhill for the handoff, takes two steps, then breaks outside around the end to follow the motion back.

Q – Reverses out and hands off to the deep back. Q then shows pass.

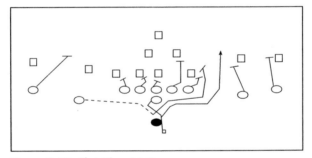

Figure 7-13. Slot Rip—64 Bounce

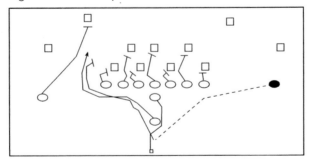

Figure 7-14. Flanker Lou—45 Bounce

46 AND 47 POWER

46 and 47 Power are power plays for the back in motion. As the offensive line blocks down, the fullback load blocks on the last man on the line of scrimmage. The backside guard OG blocks for the motion back off-tackle. You can also call 26 and 27 Power or 66 and 67 Power (Figures 7-15 and 7-16).

Rules for 46 and 47 Power:

PT/PG/C – Combo down block to the inside.

BG – OG blocks and leads off-tackle into the hole for the motion back.

BT – Sets inside and pretends to pass block.

PTE – Combo blocks inside to linebacker.

BTE – Releases for free safety.

MB – Goes into short motion, releases laterally to the side called, as if he is going to receive a pitch, then comes hard towards the outside leg of the playside tackle for the handoff. The motion back follows the backside guard into the hole and cuts off his block.

F – Load blocks the last man on the line of scrimmage.

Q – Opens at a 45-degree angle deep over the playside tackle to hand off to the motion back. The quarterback then continues back and sets up as if to pass.

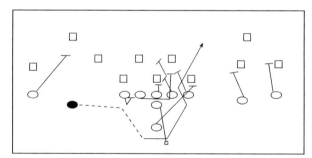

Figure 7-15. Slot Roy—46 Power

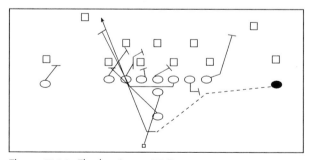

Figure 7-16. Flanker Lou—47 Power

46 AND 47 COUNTER

46 and 47 Counter are off-tackle misdirection plays for the motion back. The fullback goes in the opposite direction as the backside guard and tackle pull to block for the motion back (Figures 7-17 and 7-18).

Rules for 46 and 47 Counter:

PT/PG/C – Down block to the inside.

BG – Pulls playside to kick-out or roll block the last defender on the line of scrimmage.

BT – Follows the backside guard and reads his block. If the backside guard kicks out the last defender on the line of scrimmage, the backside tackle cuts underneath and lead blocks for the ball carrier. If the backside guard roll blocks his defender, the backside tackle comes around and still leads for the runner.

TEs – Playside or backside block down inside to C gap.

SE/B – Base/stalk block their defender.

MB – Goes in short or medium motion. In short motion, the motion back takes a hop step in the opposite direction, then comes back downhill for the handoff from the quarterback. The motion back cuts off the backside tackle's lead block.

F – Comes hard at the outside hip of the backside tackle to stop pursuit.

Q – Opens away from the hole at a 45-degree angle, then breaks back and hands off to the motion back off his inside hip. The quarterback then bootlegs to the side he opened.

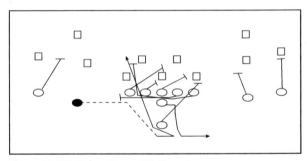

Figure 7-17. Twins Roy—47 Counter

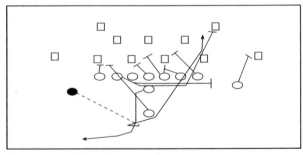

Figure 7-18. Wing Roy—46 Counter

48 AND 49 ZONE

48 and 49 Zone are designed tosses to the motion back. The line zone blocks playside and the fullback blocks force. The ballcarrier tries to get outside, but cuts back at the first opportunity (Figures 7-19 and 7-20).

Rules for 48 and 49 Zone:

Line/TEs – Zone block to the side called.

PTE – Must try to hook block the last man on the line of scrimmage. PTE can go to the next level, but not until the playside tackle has taken over his block.

PT – Zones hard playside and reaches PTE's defender to take over his block. If PT cannot reach the defender by the third step, he turns up field to cut off linebackers.

SE/B – Stalk/base block.

MB – Goes in short motion. Releases laterally for the toss and reads the fullback's block.

F – Lead blocks for the motion back. The fullback cut blocks first threat.

Q – Reverses out and pitches to the motion back. The quarterback continues playside to provide additional protection, or may bootleg.

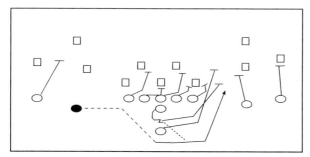

Figure 7-19. Twins Roy—48 Zone

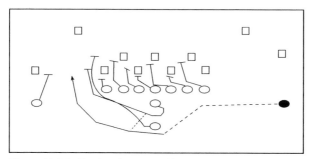

Figure 7-20. Flanker Lou—49 Zone

48 AND 49 GOG

48 and 49 GOG are designed tosses for the motion back. Both guards pull and the fullback attacks the playside linebacker (Figures 7-21 and 7-22).

Rules for 48 and 49 GOG:

PT – Blocks down if uncovered, or hook blocks if covered.

PG – Pulls playside and cut blocks force man. If both the playside tackle and guard are covered, PG stays in and zone blocks, unless a center reach block is called.

C – Blocks down if uncovered; zone blocks if covered.

BG – Pulls playside and looks to cut up field when he nears the playside tackle's position.

PTE – Hook blocks.

BTE – Zones playside to the safety.

MB – Takes the toss and tries to get to the outside. The ballcarrier should look to cut back against the flow.

SE/B – Stalk block.

F – Attacks the playside linebacker with a cut block. Does not allow any linebacker to come underneath the pulling guards.

Q – Reverses out and pitches to the motion back. Q continues playside to cut off pursuit.

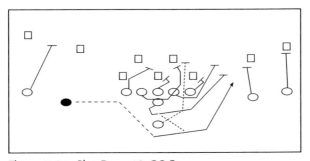

Figure 7-21. Slot Roy—48 GOG

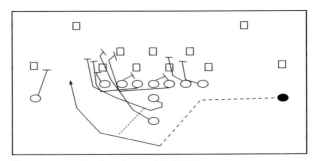

Figure 7-22. Flanker Lou—49 GOG

62 AND 63 LEAD DRAW

62 and 63 Lead Draw are draws to the tailback with the medium motion back as the lead blocker. The offensive line follows the lead blocking rules with one backward toe-heel step (Figures 7-23 and 7-24).

Rules for 62 and 63 Lead Draw:

Offensive line – Follows the lead rules with one exception. The line takes one quick back step to invite the rushers up field. They should not open towards the hole, and should try to keep their butts to the hole.

SE/B – Run defenders off and stalk block.

TEs – Run defenders off and stalk block.

MB – Goes in medium motion. On the snap, the motion back takes a jab step away from the hole, but plants and comes back for the lead block on the playside linebacker.

T – Takes one lateral step and counts *one* before coming downhill for the quarterback's handoff. The tailback reads the motion back's block and runs for daylight.

Q – Opens playside and comes back to hand off to the tailback.

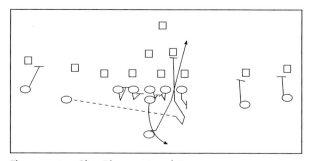

Figure 7-23. Slot Rip—62 Lead Draw

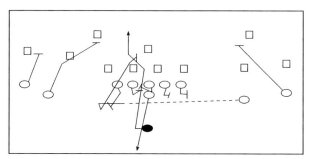

Figure 7-24. Twins Lip—63 Lead Draw

CHAPTER 8

Play-Action Pass

The play-action pass is important to any offense. If the running game is having success, the play-action pass can be a back breaker. A strong running team can go the entire season without a dropback pass, but they should still have the play-action pass to keep the defense honest.

When calling play-action passes, call the type of running-back action with the receivers' routes. To call the back action, place the number 1 in front of the series or use the words, *pass, dump,* or *bootleg.* The receivers' routes are usually given at the end of the play, except for the bootlegs. Bootlegs and Power Passes use the levels combination. Calling the routes tells everyone exactly where to go and provides the flexibility to change the routes. For example, if the play-action pass is off the inside-veer action, call "Roy – 1 - 14-74." If the play-action pass is off the lead action, call "Roy - 42 Lead Pass - 7D8."

Levels is a predetermined route combination discussed in Chapter 2. The playside outside receiver runs an 8 route (Flag). If you have a second playside receiver, he runs a 4 route (Out). Backside receivers run drags and posts. If the fullback is not the back making the fake, he is in the playside flat. On Bootlegs and Power Pass, you can still give route combinations, for example, 26 Bootleg 68.

The running backs, quarterback, and offensive line must sell the play-action pass. The backs must carry out their fakes as the offensive line sells the run without going downfield. If the tight ends chip/delay block, they must sell the run first to bring the safeties up.

The spread option offense uses play-action passes off the inside-veer action, outside-veer action, lead action, power action, and counter action. You can attack towards motion and also away from motion.

Each pass is broken down into different types of reads. The reads will consist of a presnap, position, progression, or a combination of each.

PLAY-ACTION PASS LIST

- 1-14-74 or 1-15-74
- 1-14-48 or 1-15-48
- 1-16-7FL or 1-17-7FL
- 1-16-7LF or 1-17-7LF
- 1-44-7D8 OG Left or 1-45-7D8 OG Right
- 46 and 47 Power Pass
- 26 and 27 Bootleg
- 47 and 48 Bootleg

DIAGRAM KEY

··················	Primary receiver
———	Receiver (presnap)
- - - - -	Secondary routes

IN PASS

1-14/15-74 and 1-14/15-48 are play-action passes off the inside-veer action (Figures 8-1 and 8-2).

Rules for In Pass:

Line – Steps hard towards the playside and jab blocks. Uncovered linemen need to stay on the line of scrimmage and check for linebackers as they help the covered lineman. If uncovered, the playside tackle steps hard playside at the defender over the tight end. After checking first for a middle blitz, the uncovered backside guard or center can peel back to block a backside linebacker blitz.

First Receiver – Runs a 7 (Rub) route on 1-14/15-74, or runs a 4 route on 1-14/15-48.

Second Receiver – Runs a 4 route on 1-14/15-74, or runs an 8 route on 1-14/15-48.

MB – Goes in short motion and bubbles out wide as a secondary receiver.

Backside Split End – Runs the hot slant or fade depending on the coverage.

F – Dives hard at the hole called for a fake handoff. The fullback must come hard into the line of scrimmage to have the linebacker(s) step up.

Q – Fakes to the fullback and takes two back steps. The 74 combination route is a progression read in which the 7 route rubs for the 4 route. Q reads the 4 route, then the 7 route. If the coverage is 0, Q can throw the 7 route first. The 48 combination route is a position read on the cornerback. The quarterback throws the 8 route if the corner is up, or the 4 route if the corner is deep. Note: The quarterback will throw the automatic slant/fade to the backside end if the backside linebacker blitzes. Q can throw the bubble to the back as another secondary route.

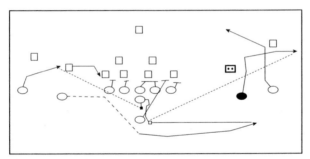

Figure 8-1. Twins Roy—1-14-74

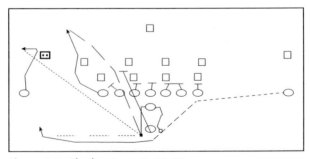

Figure 8-2. Flanker Lou—1-15-48

OUT PASS

1-16/17-7FL and 1-16/17-7LF are play-action passes off the outside veer action with three receivers to one side (Figures 8-3 and 8-4).

Rules for Out Pass:

Line – Steps hard towards the playside and jab blocks. If uncovered, the playside tackle steps hard playside at the defender over the tight end. After checking first for a middle blitz, the uncovered backside guard or center can peel back to block a backside linebacker blitz.

BTE – Stays in to block, unless given a fourth number.

First Receiver – Runs a skinny 7 route on 1-16/17-7FL/7LF. The 7 route can sit down if coverage is deep.

Second Receiver – Runs an F route on 1-16/17-7FL, or runs an L route on 1-16/17-7LF.

MB – Runs the L route on 7FL, and the F route on 7LF.

SE/B – Run a read route depending on the coverage.

F – Dives hard at the outside hip of the playside tackle as if to get the football, then chop blocks the last man on the line of scrimmage.

Q – Checks presnap reaction to motion. If the backside linebacker comes, the backside read route is hot. 7LF is a position read. Another presnap read is the L route. As Q opens laterally two steps while faking to the fullback, Q checks the L. He then takes two steps back and reads the position of the outside linebacker or strong safety. Q throws the 7 if the position read jumps the F, or throws the F if the position read drops into coverage.

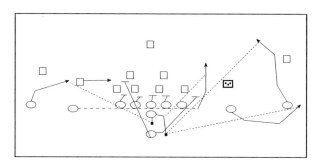

Figure 8-3. Slot Rip—1-16-7FL

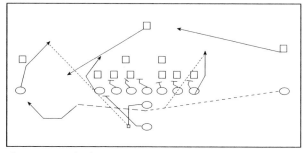

Figure 8-4. Flanker Larry—1-17-7LF

LEAD PASS

1-44-7D8 and 1-45-7D8 are progression play-action passes off the lead-power action with an OG backside protection block (Figures 8-5 and 8-6).

Rules for Lead Pass:

Line – The playside guard OG blocks to the backside to protect the quarterback's blind spot. The center must block back if uncovered. The rest of the line will pass block aggressively.

First Receiver – Runs a 7 route. This is a three-move post route.

Second Receiver – Runs a D route underneath the coverage.

Third Receiver – Acts as the backside end. He runs an 8 route.

MB – Goes in short motion and comes hard towards the hole called for a fake handoff.

F – Fires hard at the last man on the playside to cut block. In the flanker formation, the fullback will cut the defender in front of the playside tight end.

Q – Reverses out and fakes the lead. Q has a progression read of 7-8-D. If the coverage is 0, the quarterback's presnap read is the 7. In cover 1, he reads the 8 route then checks the D route dragging across to weakside. On cover zero, Q may only have the D route open.

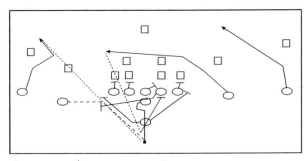

Figure 8-5. Slot Roy—1-44-7D8

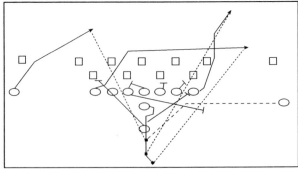

Figure 8-6. Flanker Roy—1-45-7D8

POWER PASS

46 and 47 Power Pass are strong goal-line plays because the outside linebacker is usually aggressive against the run. The quarterback fakes to the motion back on the power action and then checks level routes (Figures 8-7 and 8-8).

Rules for Power Pass:

Line – Aggressively pass blocks with the backside guard pulling playside. The center blocks back if uncovered.

Receivers – Run the levels system. Widest playside receiver runs the 8 route. The second playside receiver runs a 4 route. The third receiver, or fullback, runs a 2 route. Any backside tight end or slot receiver runs a D route. The backside split end runs a 7 route.

PTE – Releases inside before running his route.

MB – Goes in short motion and fakes the power to the side called.

F – Fires hard at the playside tight-end position. The fullback hits the defender in front of the playside tight end and then releases into the flat for a 2 route.

Q – Opens playside as if to hand off on the power, but fakes instead and takes two additional steps behind the fake. In this progression/position read versus cover 1, the quarterback's first read is deep for the 8 route by checking the cornerback's position. If the cornerback is even or behind the 8 route, Q throws the deep 8 route. If the cornerback is deep, Q throws the 4 medium route, unless he sees a strong under coverage. In that situation, Q must throw to the fullback's 2 route or run the ball.

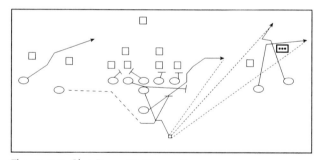

Figure 8-7. Slot Roy—46 Power Pass

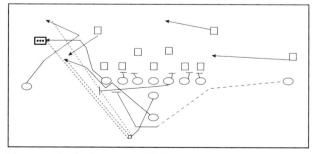

Figure 8-8. Flanker Lou—47 Power Pass

26 AND 27 BOOTLEG

26/27 and 66/67 Bootleg are counter-action bootleg passes with an OG block (Figures 8-9 and 8-10).

Rules for 26 and 27 Bootleg:

Line – Aggressively pass blocks with the backside guard pulling playside. The center blocks down if uncovered. The right guard pulls to the left on 26 Bootleg, as the left guard pulls to the right on 27 Bootleg.

Receivers – Run the levels system. The widest playside receiver runs the 8 route. The second playside receiver runs a 4 route. The third receiver in medium motion runs a 2 delay route, after chipping the defensive end. Any backside tight end or slot receiver runs a D route. The backside split end runs a 7 route.

F/PT/BT – Fake the counter and block backside pressure.

Q – Opens to the side of the bootleg and fakes to the fullback on the counter action. The quarterback bootlegs and first position reads the cornerback for the deep 8 route, and then for the 4 route. If these routes are covered, or the quarterback feels too much pressure, he throws to the motion man's 2 route or runs the ball. The quarterback also has a secondary option of any D and 7 routes from the backside against zero coverage.

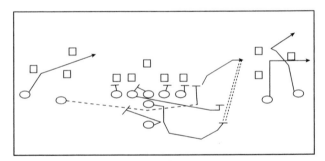

Figure 8-9. Slot Rip—27 Bootleg

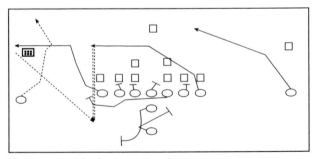

Figure 8-10. Flanker—26 Bootleg

46 AND 47 BOOTLEG

46 and 47 Bootleg are play-action passes off the counter action with the backside guard pulling on an OG block (Figures 8-11 and 8-12).

Rules for 46 and 47 Bootleg:

Line – Aggressively pass blocks with the backside guard pulling playside. The center needs to block back if uncovered. The right guard pulls to the left on 46 Bootleg, as the left guard pulls to the right on 47 Bootleg.

Receivers – Run the levels system. The widest playside receiver runs the 8 route. The second playside receiver runs a 4 route. The third receiver, or fullback, runs a 2 delay route after he chips the last man on the line of scrimmage. Any backside tight end or slot receiver runs a D route. The backside split end runs a 7 route.

MB – Goes in short motion and fakes the counter. He blocks backside pressure.

F – Goes hard at the last man on the playside line of scrimmage and hits him on the outside shoulder. He then releases into the flat on a 2 route. F is a hot receiver.

Q – Opens to the side of the bootleg and fakes to the motion back on the counter action. The quarterback bootlegs and first reads the position of the cornerback for the 8 route (first outside receiver), and 4 route (the second receiver). If these routes are covered, or the quarterback feels too much pressure, he throws the fullback's 2 route. The quarterback also has the secondary option of any D and 7 routes from the backside.

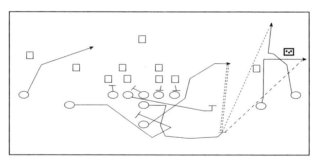

Figure 8-11. Slot Roy—47 Bootleg

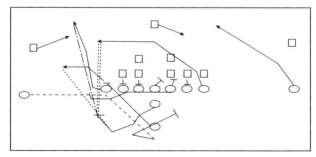

Figure 8-12. Flanker Roy—46 Bootleg

CHAPTER 9

Passing Series

This chapter addresses the pass combinations from the Quick (30 Series), Stop (50 Series), and Fan (70 Series) Passing Series. In all of these plays, the offensive line blocks Big on Big and the one back blocks Back on Back. This chapter also discusses mirror routes in balanced formations, three-route combinations in trips formations, and four-route combinations.

In mirror routes, only two numbers/letters are given. The first number/letter is for the outside receiver, and the second number/letter is for the second receiver. Three-receiver route combinations are used in trips formations. The man in motion runs the third route called. If the backside receiver is a split end, he runs a slant or a fade. This is one of the quarterback's presnap hot receivers. If the backside receiver is a tight end, he stays in to block unless the quarterback gives a fourth number. The Quick Check-With-Me series can also use three receivers.

Four-route combinations are called with four numbers left to right in two combinations. The first two numbers apply to the left pair of receivers, and the second pair of numbers applies to the two receivers to the right. Usually one pair will be designed for cover 1 and the other pair will be for cover 2, for example, 5D-48 Scat.

Words can also represent a combination of routes. For example, if you call slot, Bootleg Right, and do not give any routes, the receivers run the levels system.

QUICK – 30 SERIES

In the quick passing series, the quarterback takes one drop-step with the pop step. The quick series uses routes 0, 1, 2, 3, and F. The 0, 1, and 2 routes can be thrown with just one step. The pop step is a heel-to-heel shuffle that takes the quarterback away from the line of scrimmage and helps him gather his feet together before delivery. He does not take a crossover step to throw.

The offensive line can chop or jab block on defenders inside out. If the fullback/tailback is back deep behind the quarterback, he may have to shift up and close to the left A gap to help block.

Quick also refers to the 30 Series (30, 31, 32, and 33). If the play is called "Quick Check-With-Me," the quarterback calls one of the four 30 Series depending on his presnap read. Because he should throw the ball in less than two seconds, the quarterback checks for defensive backs in a poor alignment for the called routes. The one-column numbers of the 30 Series represent the first route of the widest receiver. The second receiver must remember his complementary route. This chapter discusses the following four mirror examples: Quick 01 (30), Quick 10 (31), Quick 25 (32), and Quick 33 (33).

All trips-combination routes are usually called in the huddle. Each of the four quick series can also motion into a trips formation. Unless the routes are given, the motion man and second receiver must remember their complementary routes. The quarterback may audible to a quick-trips combination. By tapping the side of his leg, the quarterback tells the motion man you have a trips combination. The motion man must know his alignment on the following four quick trips combinations: Quick 012 (30), Quick 107 (31), Quick 250 (32), and Quick 38D (33).

STOP – 50 SERIES

Stop tells the offensive linemen to take one heel-toe step backward before pulling their guns to Big on Big pass protect. The quarterback takes a three-step dropback with a pop step timed for intermediate routes. These intermediate routes only use one or two moves (out, curl, post, and flag). The quarterback must be ready to throw off their breaks. Stop is also called by the 50 Series.

Stop combinations (50 Series) are effective because the quarterback throws the ball quickly without giving the opponent the opportunity to sack him. The quarterback must follow two rules when passing: First, no interceptions, and second, no sacks! If the quarterback sees a rusher will be unblocked, he can always check for the hot route or change the play to a 30 Series.

Many of the reads in the stop combinations are progression or position reads. A progression read tells the quarterback that a certain receiver, versus a particular secondary coverage, should be open first. Several progression reads use some type of man or zone pick. These become the primary reads. Secondary reads come from the routes that open after the picks or from a change in the secondary coverage. Do not try to have three reads after the snap of the ball. Instead, throw the ball away.

A position read tells the quarterback to read a particular defensive back. As the quarterback takes his three dropback steps, he watches the reaction of the position read. As the quarterback hits his pop step, he must decide which direction to throw. This is an area-type pass because the defender is not in that location.

The 50 Series (stop combinations) consist of the following: Stop 48 (54), Stop 55 (55), Stop 74 (57), and Stop 872 (58). If the play is Stop Check-With-Me, the quarterback can call one of these four combinations. If the defense is sending a seven-man rush against six blockers, the quarterback must audible to a 30 Series.

Stop, like the Quick Series, can use trips combinations. The man in motion has a complementary route. Usually these trips combinations are called in the huddle. The complementary routes for the four-stop combinations are Stop 483 (54), Stop 550 (55), Stop 74D (57), and Stop 872 (58).

Short motion in stop combinations is also used in the Passing Series. Many opponents will believe short motion means run! But short motion also means an extra blocker for pass protection. The motion back comes into the I formation, and on the snap, he checks to the frontside for backers inside out. The fullback does the same on the backside. In stop or fan combinations, the quarterback can always hand signal behind him for scat and scoot routes for the one back.

FAN – 70 SERIES

Fan tells the offensive line to take two heel-to-heel steps backward as they punch and extend their arms. The blocking rule is still Big on Big. This dropback pass is the most difficult because of the time needed to throw the ball. Call this five step dropback (with a pop step) in third and long situations because everyone knows the high probability for a pass. The risk of a sack is higher, but that does not matter because it is already third and long.

In the fan combinations, routes that will attack the middle versus cover 2 are best. These routes could be progression or position reads. If the defense is going to rush an extra defender, the quarterback must change the play to a 30 or 50 Series because of the depth of many of these routes. You can also call the fan combinations in the 70 Series, using the following: Fan 68 (76), Fan 78 (77), Fan 86 (78), and Fan 9S (79) for mirror routes; and Fan 685 (76), Fan 784 (77), Fan 86C (78), and Fan 9S7 (79) for trips combinations.

BIG ON BIG

Quick, stop, and fan use the same blocking scheme: Big on Big. A covered lineman blocks his defender. An uncovered lineman checks for a blitzing linebacker as he helps his partner double-team. If the middle linebackers are stacked over the guards, the center and fullback check right and left for blitz. The fullback checks the middle for an outside linebacker. Short motion and backside tackle against trips will usually stay in to block for max protection (Figures 9-1 through 9-4).

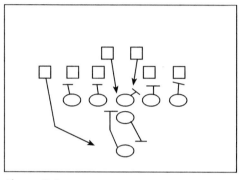

Figure 9-1

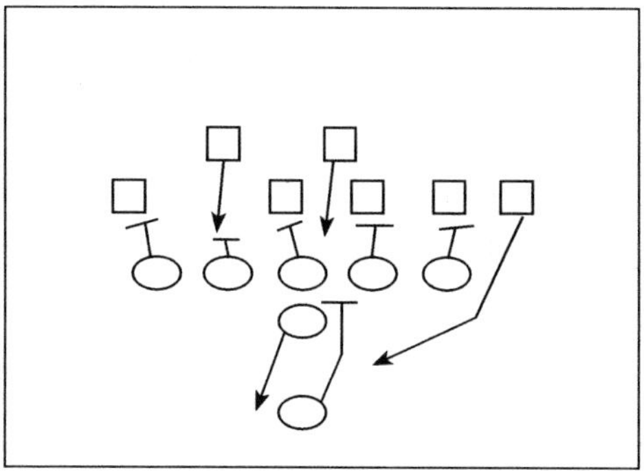

Figure 9-2

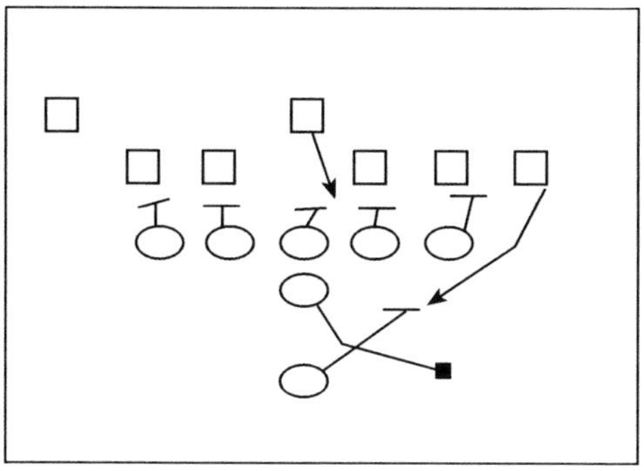

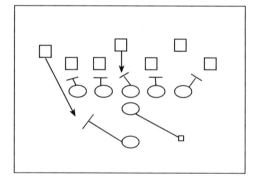

Figure 9-3

Figure 9-4

ROUTES RELEASES AND STEPS

- O/Fade – Releases outside and deep. Receivers look for the ball quickly as they are up the sideline.

- 1/Slant – Releases inside for two steps then breaks hard at 45-degree angle.

- 2/Flat – Releases outside and up for three steps (5 yards). The 2 then breaks outside at a 90 degree angle.

- 3/Hook – Releases slightly inside and up for three hard steps (5 yards). The 3 route then turns sharply inside for ball.

- 4/Out – Releases outside for five to six steps (8 to 10 yards). The 4 route plants with the inside foot and cuts at a 90-degree angle towards the sideline. The 4 route must be ready for the ball off the break.

- 5/Curl – Releases outside for five to six steps (8 to 10 yards). The 5 route then turns sharply inside looking for the ball.

- 6/Comeback – Releases outside as if the receiver is running a fade. At 16 to 17 yards, the 6 route plants with the inside leg and comes back to the sideline at a 45 degree angle for the pass.

- 7/Post – Releases inside for five hard steps. The 7 can give an outside fake and then cut slightly inside towards the post.

- 8/Flag – Releases inside or straight up for five hard steps (8 to 10 yards). The 8 then breaks hard inside for two steps before breaking back to the outside for the flag.

- 9/Post Corner – Releases inside and runs a hard post to 16/17 yards. The 9 then plants and comes back to the middle of the field.

- F/Flair – Releases laterally on a bubble route.

- Bench – Releases inside as if running a slant route. The Bench then breaks outside at about 8 yards to run a corner route. At 17 to 20 yards, the receiver breaks back to the sideline as if he was running a comeback.

- C/Cross – Releases deep up field for 15 yards. The receiver plants and then crosses the middle in order to find a hole deep to sit into.

- D/Drag – Releases inside and runs across the field climbing his route 10 to 15 yards deep. D must be under control for pass thrown behind.

- L/Look – Looks over his inside shoulder by his second step.

- S/Out and Up – Breaks outside as if he is going to run a flat, then quickly breaks up the sideline deep.

SCAT/SCOOT

In some cases, instead of having the fullback stay in to block, you want him to go to the right or left side. *Scat* tells the one back to go to the left and *Scoot* tells him to go to the right. Call Stop 5D-48 Scat or Stop 48-5D Scoot in the huddle. This is a four-receiver route combination with the fullback running a bubble route instead of staying in to block the backer. The quarterback can also signal for scat or scoot on any combination by pointing behind his back. Figures 9-5 and 9-6 illustrate Stop 5D-48 Scat and Stop 48-5D Scoot.

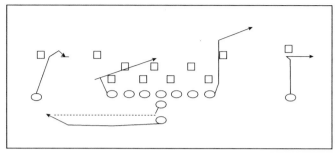

Figure 9-5. Flanker—Stop 5D-48 (Left Flanker - 5, Left Tight End - D, Right Flanker - 4, Right Tight End - 8, F - Scat)

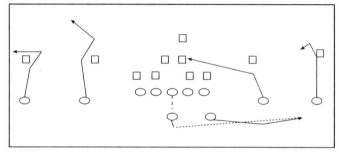

Figure 9-6. Gun Slot—Stop 48-5D Scoot (Left SE - 4, Left Slot - 8, Right SE - 5, Right Slot - D, F - Scoot)

HOT, PRIMARY, AND SECONDARY RECEIVERS

The hot receiver is the quarterback's first objective. He uses a presnap read for the quick routes (0, 1, 2, and 3). The hot routes are designed to hurt the different types of blitzes.

The primary receiver is the quarterback's main objective in a route combination. The route(s) could be position or progression reads. On the position read(s), there may be two primary receivers. This tells the quarterback he can throw to either receiver depending on the reaction to the position read (Figure 9-7).

On progression reads, which are usually rubs, the quarterback keys that receiver first unless the secondary is in a different alignment. The quarterback can change the play or go to his secondary route for a particular coverage. If the hot and primary receivers are covered, the secondary receiver is the last read for the quarterback. Many secondary receiver routes are designed to hurt cover 2. After the secondary read, the quarterback must throw the ball away or scramble, depending on the down and distance.

Diagram Key:

.... Hot routes

▥ Position read

- - - - - Primary routes

● Rub receiver

::::::::: Secondary routes

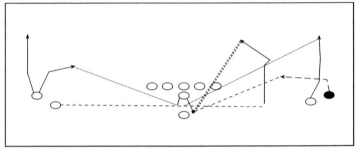

Figure 9-7. Twins Rip—Quick 107 (Left SE - Hot Read Route, Left Slot - Secondary 7 Route, Right Slot - Hot 0 Route, Right SE - Primary Rub 1 Route)

LEVELS

Levels was discussed in Chapter 8. Levels tells the quarterback to read the cornerback's position and work top to bottom. This combination is usually on the bootleg and power passes. Bootleg out of the shotgun is a good call. The first playside receiver runs a flag. The second playside receiver runs an out. The back out or motion man runs a flat. All backside backs and receivers drag and post.

Levels does not have a true hot receiver, but the fullback should open quickly out of the gun. In cover 1, the quarterback can position read the playside corner. In cover 2, the primary receiver will run the out or drag routes. Figure 9-8 illustrates an example of levels in a bootleg without motion.

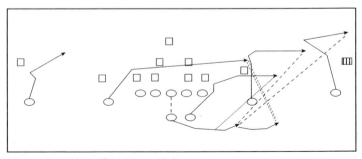

Figure 9-8. Gun Slot—Boot Right

QUICK – 30 SERIES

Quick 01 (30)

Slot—Quick 01 vs. Zero (Figure 9-9)
Presnap Read (Mismatches/Body Position/All Receivers Hot)
Note: No Secondary Receiver

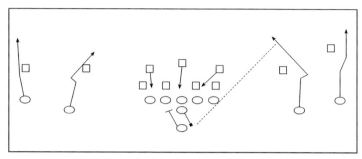

Figure 9-9. Slot—Quick 01 vs. Zero

Flanker—Larry—Quick 072 vs. One Zone (Figure 9-10)
Progression Read in Trips (2 Route then 7 Route)
Position Read – (Outside Linebacker/Strong Safety)
Note: BTE - Max Protection

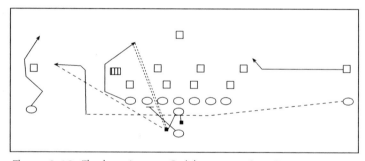

Figure 9-10. Flanker—Larry —Quick 072 vs. One Zone

Slot—Quick 01 Scoot vs. Two Man (Figure 9-11)
Progression Read (1 Route then One Back's Flare)
Position Read (Outside Linebackers on Scoot Side)

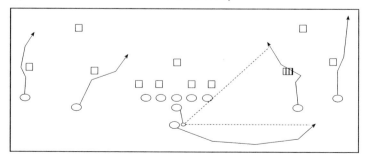

Figure 9-11. Slot—Quick 01 Scoot vs. Two Man

Quick 10 (31)

Twins—Quick 10 vs. Lose Zero (Figure 9-12)
Presnap Read (Body Position/Slant Jumping Corners/All Receivers Hot)
Note: No Secondary Read

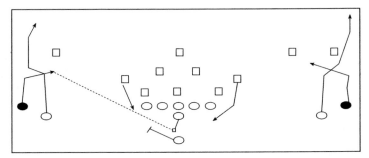

Figure 9-12. Twins —Quick 10 vs. Lose Zero

Slot —Lip—Quick 107 vs. One Man (Figure 9-13)
Progression Read (1 Route then 7 Route)
Position Read (Outside Linebacker/Strong Safety)

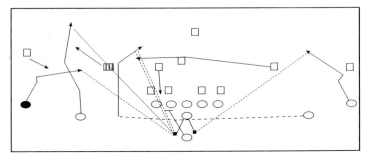

Figure 9-13. Slot—Lip—Quick 107 vs. One Man

Flanker—Rip—Quick 107 Dump Weak vs. Two Zone (Figure 9-14)
Secondary Position Read (Read Middle Backer for One Back's Dump or 7 Route)

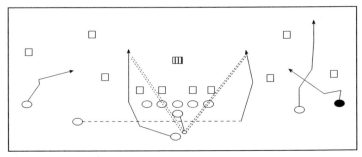

Figure 9-14. Flanker —Rip—Quick 107 Dump Weak vs. Two Zone

Quick 250 (32)

Slot—Rover—Quick 250 vs. Zero Rotate (Figure 9-15)
Presnap and Position Read (Playside Corner)
Progression Read (2 Route then 5 Route)

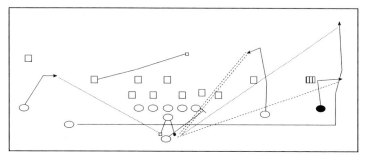

Figure 9-15. Slot—Rover—Quick 250 vs. Zero Rotate

Flanker—Quick 25 vs. One Zone (Figure 9-16)
Progression Read (2 Route then 5 Route)
Note: The unpicked 2 Route is also the hot route.

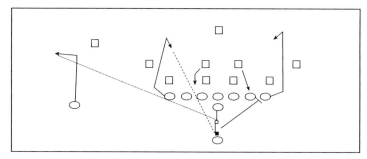

Figure 9-16. Flanker—Quick 25 vs. One Zone

Flanker—Rover—Quick 250 Scoot (Figure 9-17)
Progression Read vs. Two (5 Route then One Back's Scoot)

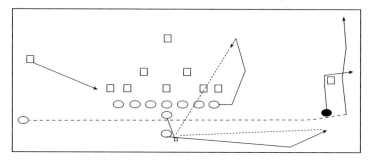

Figure 9-17. Flanker—Rover—Quick 250 Scoot

Quick 38 (33)

Slot—Reggie—Quick vs. Zero (Figure 9-18)
Presnap Read—(3 Route is hot.)
Progression Read (3 Route then 8 Route)

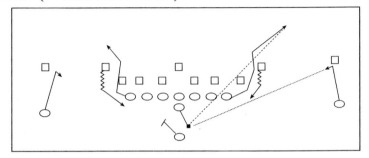

Figure 9-18. Slot—Reggie—Quick vs. Zero

Quick BBF

Slot—Reggie—Quick BBF vs. One Zone (Figure 9-19)
Presnap Read (Secondary's reaction to motion)
Primary Receiver – (F Route)

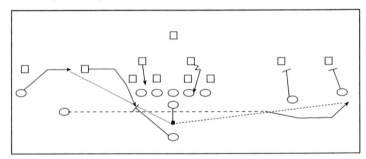

Figure 9-19. Slot—Reggie—Quick BBF vs. One Zone

Quick X Slant-Go

Quick Reggie X Slant-Go (Figure 9-20)
Position Read (Backside Corner)
Progression Read (1 Go Route to Drag Route)
Note: Q pump fakes and slides back. No hot route.

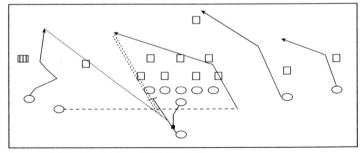

Figure 9-20. Quick Reggie X Slant-Go

STOP – 50 SERIES

Stop 54 (54)

Slot—Stop 48 vs. Zero with Deep Linebackers (Figure 9-21)
Position Read (Cornerback)
Note: No hot read.

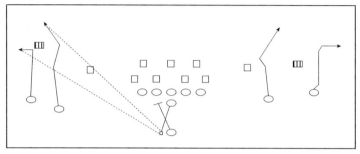

Figure 9-21. Slot—Stop 48 vs. Zero with Deep Linebackers

Flanker—Stop 48 Delay Right (Figure 9-22)
Position Read (Cornerback)
Secondary Read – (Fullback Delay)
Note: No hot read.

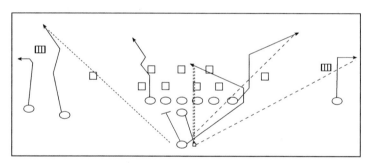

Figure 9-22. Flanker—Stop 48 Delay Right

Twin—Reggie—Stop 485 Dump Right vs. Two Zone (Figure 9-23)
Progression Read vs. Cover 2 (FB's Dump then Motion Man's 5 Route)

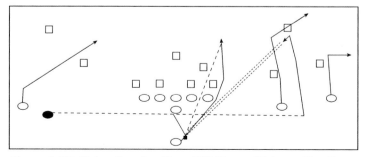

Figure 9-23. Twin—Reggie—Stop 485 Dump Right vs. Two Zone

Stop 55 (55)

Flanker—Stop 55 Scat vs. Zero and 7 Man Rush (Figure 9-24)
Presnap Read (Mismatches/Body Position)
Progression Read (TE's 5 Route and then Scat Route)
Note: Scat could also be hot read.

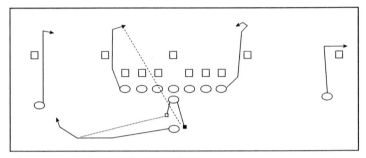

Figure 9-24. Flanker—Stop 55 Scat vs. Zero and 7 Man Rush

Slot—Reggie—Stop 550 vs. One Man (Figure 9-25)
Progression Read (Outside Pick for 5 Route then Inside 5 Route)
Position Read (Cornerback)

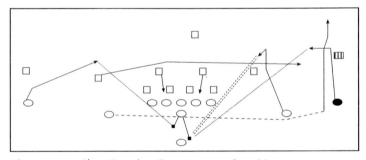

Figure 9-25. Slot—Reggie—Stop 550 vs. One Man

Slot—Rip—Stop 550 vs. Two Zone (Figure 9-26)
Progression Read (Inside Pick for 5 Route then Outside 5 Route)
Position Read (Outside Linebacker)

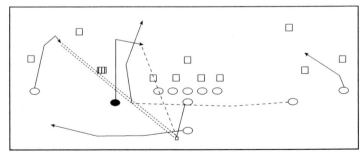

Figure 9-26. Slot—Rip—Stop 550 vs. Two Zone

Stop 74 (57)

Twins—Stop 74 vs. Zero and 6 Man Rush (Figure 9-27)
Progression Read (4 Route then 7 Route)
Position Read (Safeties)

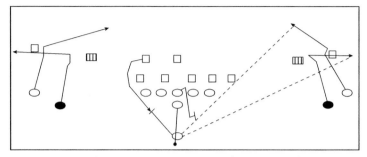

Figure 9-27. Twins—Stop 74 vs. Zero and 6 Man Rush

Twins Stop 74 Shoot Left vs. One (Figure 9-28)
Progression Read (4 Route then One Back's Shoot)
Note: Alert One Back if hot route is needed!

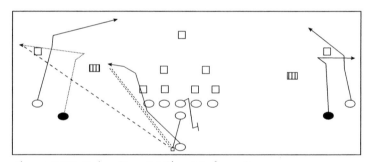

Figure 9-28. Twins Stop 74 Shoot Left vs. One

Flanker—Rip—Stop 74D vs. Two Zone (Figure 9-29)
Progression Read (4 Route then D Route)
Note: BTE - Max Protection

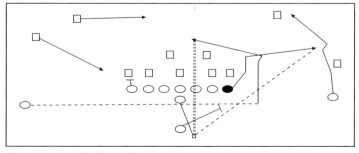

Figure 9-29. Flanker—Rip—Stop 74D vs. Two Zone

Stop 872 (58)

Slot—Rover—Stop 872 vs. Zero (Figure 9-30)
Presnap Read (Backside 1 or 2 Route)
Progression Read (8 Route then 7 Route)

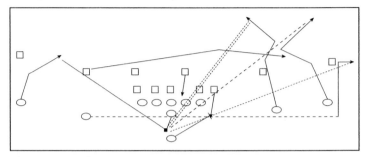

Figure 9-30. Slot—Rover—Stop 872 vs. Zero

Flanker—Rover—Stop 872 vs. One Zone (Figure 9-31)
Presnap Read (Secondary's Rotation/2 Route for Hot)
Progression Read (8 Route and then 7 Route)
Note: BTE - Max Protection

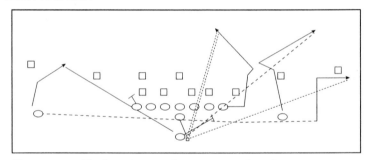

Figure 9-31. Flanker—Rover—Stop 872 vs. One Zone

Slot—Lassie—Stop 872 Delay Right vs. Two Man (Figure 9-32)
Progression Read vs. Two Deep (7 Route then Delay Route)

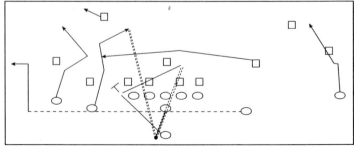

Figure 9-32. Slot—Lassie—Stop 872 Delay Right vs. Two Man

FAN – 70 SERIES

Fan 685 (76)

Flanker–Lip–Fan 685 (Figure 9-33)
Position Read (Cornerback) If cornerback sits down, thro
throw 6 route. (Flag and Comeback then Motion Man'
Note: BTE - Max Protection. No hot receiver on ei

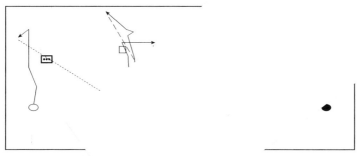

Figure 9-33. Flar.

Slot–Fan 68 Dump Left vs. One   .)
Position Read (Cornerback) Throw   .e if corner sits. (8 Route and 6 Route then
Dump Route)

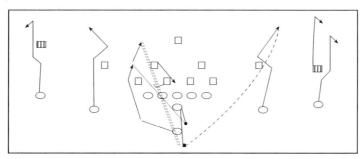

Figure 9-34. Slot—Fan 68 Dump Left vs. One

Slot–Reggie–Fan 68C (Changed the 5 Route to a C Route) (Figure 9-35)
(6 Route then C Route)

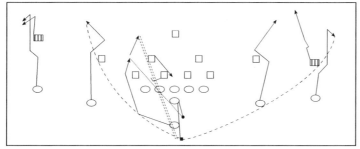

Figure 9-35. Slot—Reggie—Fan 68C (Changed the 5 Route to a
C Route)

Fan 784 (77)

Slot—Rip—Fan 784 (Figure 9-36)
Presnap Read (Backside 1 Route/Adjustment to Motion)
Position Read (Cornerback) versus zero and one deep
Progression Read (7 and 8 Route then 4 Route)

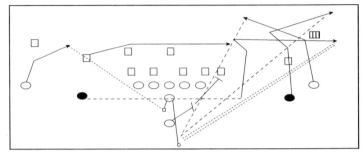

Figure 9-36. Slot—Rip—Fan 784

Flanker—Larry—Fan 748 (Figure 9-37)
Position Read (Cornerback) versus one deep
Progression Read (7 and 8 Route then 4 Route)
Note: BTE - Max Protection

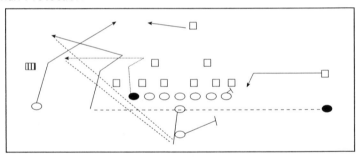

Figure 9-37. Flanker—Larry—Fan 748

Twins—Fan 78 Delay Left vs. Two Zone (Figure 9-38)
Position Read (Deep Safety)
Progression Read (7 and 8 Route then One Back Delay)

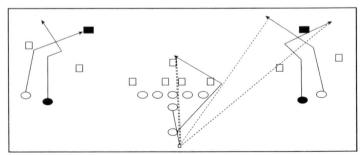

Figure 9-38. Twins—Fan 78 Delay Left vs. Two Zone

Fan 86C (78)

Flanker—Fan 86C Scoot vs. Zero (Figure 9-39)
Presnap Read (Secondary's Reaction to Motion)
Position Read (Playside Corner)
Progression Read (8 and 6 Route then C Route)

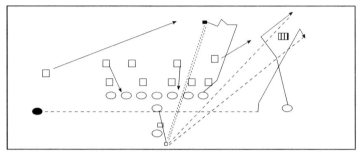

Figure 9-39. Flanker—Fan 86C Scoot vs. Zero

Slot—Fan 86 Dump Right vs. One (Figure 9-40)
Position Read (Cornerback)
Progression Read (8 and 6 Route then Dump)

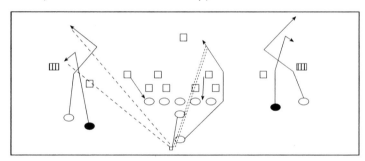

Figure 9-40. Slot—Fan 86 Dump Right vs. One

Slot—Fan 86C vs. Two Zone (Figure 9-41)
Position Read (Safety)
Progression Read (8 and 6 Route then C)

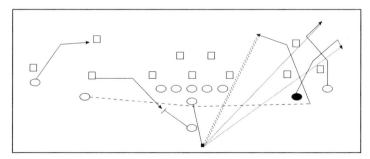

Figure 9-41. Slot—Fan 86C vs. Two Zone

Fan 9S(79)

Slot—Roy—Fan 9S vs. Zero (Figure 9-42)
Presnap Read (0 Route)
Progression Read (S Route then 9 Route)
Note: Short Motion - Extra Protection

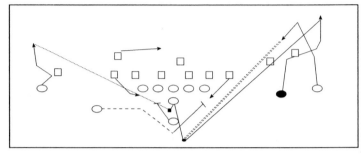

Figure 9-42. Slot—Roy—Fan 9S vs. Zero

SlotvFan 9S Scoot (Figure 9-43)
Presnap Read (Scoot)
Progression Read (S Route then 9 Route)

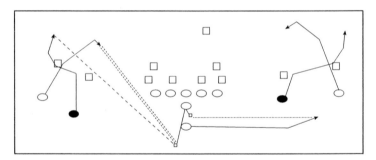

Figure 9-43. Slot—Fan 9S Scoot

Flanker—Reggie—Fan 97S vs. Two Rotate (Figure 9-44)
Progression Read (S Route and then 9 Route)
Note: BTE - Max Protection

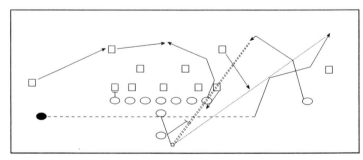

Figure 9-44. Flanker—Reggie—Fan 97S vs. Two Rotate

Boot Right Bench

Gun Right—Lip—Boot Right Bench (Figure 9-45)
Presnap Read (One Back's Flat Route)
Progression Read (Bench Route and then Drags)

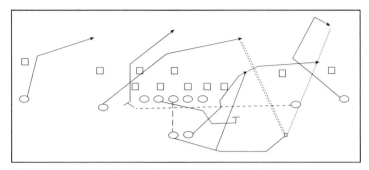

Figure 9-45. Gun Right—Lip—Boot Right Bench

Stop 5D-48 Scat/74-5D Scoot

Gun Left Stop 5D-48 Scat and Gun Right Stop 74-5D Scoot (Figure 9-46)
Presnap Read (Scat/Scoot)
Position Read vs. Cover 1 (Strong Safety on 5D Scat Combination and Cornerback vs. the 48/74 Combination)
Position Read vs. Cover 2 (Strong Safety on 5 and D, then Scat/Scoot)

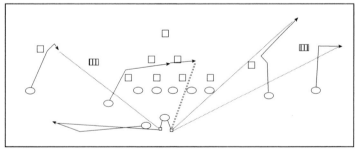

Figure 9-46. Gun Left Stop 5D-48 Scat/Gun Right Stop74-5D Scoot

Slot 48-5D Scoot (Figure 9-47)

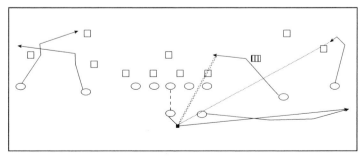

Figure 9-47. Slot 48-5D Scoot

CHAPTER 10

Screens and Draws

Screens and draws are two weapons you can use against an aggressive or soft-zone defense. They are also effective against a strong pass rush, because they cause an undisciplined defense to run past plays and slow down the pass rush.

The basic draw is called 22/23 Draw or 62/63 Lead Draw. This draw can use several different blocking schemes, including base-draw block, X-draw block, trap-draw block, and OG-draw block. Draw always tells the linemen to hinge in order to set up defenders. You can run the draw with one back, or use the quarterback.

The first type of screen is a quick hitch called GT Hitch. This quick screen is on the line of scrimmage to the split end or back. GT Hitch can be run towards the weak or strongside. The screen is called *GT* because you pull the playside guard and tackle to help block for the receiver.

The second type of screen is the outside screen called Screen Left or Screen Right. In this type of screen, the quarterback takes a full dropback to draw the rush upfield. The offensive tackles take the defensive ends outside and the guards and center block to the side called for the screen. This screen is usually to the one back or tight end.

The third type of screen is the middle screen. The middle screen uses the guards and center. The offensive tackles take a step back and push the defensive ends upfield. The middle screen uses the fullback/one back most of the time, but you can also use the slot receiver coming into the middle.

The fourth screen is a quick-split end screen that attacks the alleys and is usually run out of the gun. The quarterback has a choice between the quick-split end coming laterally behind the line of scrimmage for a quick screen, or the one back running a bubble route. The playside slot, tackle, and guard provide protection.

Draw Play List:	Screen Play List:
20/21 Trap Draw	GT Hitch
22/23 X Draw	Outside Screen
22/23 OG Draw	Middle Screen
62/63 Lead Draw (See Chapter 7)	Split-End Quick Screen

---

20 AND 21 TRAP DRAW

20 and 21 Trap Draw is a fullback draw using the trap-blocking scheme. This trap draw can be run towards or away from motion (Figures 10-1 through 10-3).

Rules for 20 and 21 Trap Draw:

PT – Takes a set step, then comes hard inside to playside linebacker on PG's *you* call. If PG calls *me*, PT runs the end upfield.

PG – Takes a set step and comes hard inside on any defender in the A gap, combo blocks with covered center, releases inside for backside linebacker. Or, influences a 2 technique on a *you* call. On *me* call, PG takes a quick-set step and attacks the middle backer.

C – If covered, takes a set step and combo blocks with the backside guard. If uncovered, he blocks down.

BG – Takes a set step and then trap blocks first defender head-up or past the playside guard.

BT – Takes a set step before he base blocks.

SE/B/TE – Base/stalk blocks.

MB – Stalk blocks.

F – Takes a slide 90-degree lateral step away from the side called. F then comes downhill to take the handoff underneath the trap block.

Q – Opens opposite the hole called and comes back to hand the ball to F.

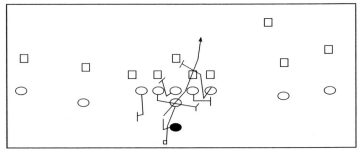

Figure 10-1. Slot—20 Trap Draw Right

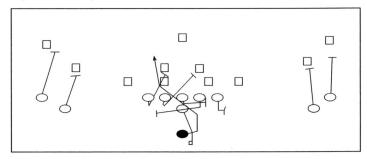

Figure 10-2. Figure—21 Trap Draw Left

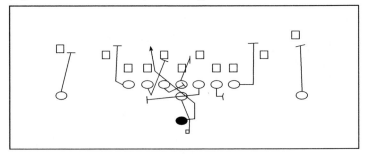

Figure 10-3. Twins—21 Trap Left

22 AND 23 X DRAW

22 and 23 Draw is a fullback draw off the dropback action. This draw uses an X Block to the playside or backside. This draw can also use the tailback, 62/63 (Figures 10-4 and 10-5).

Rules for 22 and 23 X Draw:

Line – Raises up as if to pass block and then blocks their defenders away from the hole. The front or backside guard and center execute an X block. The uncovered lineman down blocks on the covered lineman. The covered lineman then pulls around for the linebacker. If the side of the X block is not given in the huddle, it will always be to the left on 22/62 or to the right on 23/63.

SE/B/TE – Run defenders off and then stalk block.

MB – Goes in long or extra-long motion to run off and/or stalk block.

F/T – Raises up and steps to the side called. The fullback waits for the ball, then cuts toward the X block and looks for daylight. The X block is usually opposite, but can also be playside.

Q – Opens to the side called and gives the ball to the fullback. The quarterback then continues away in the same direction.

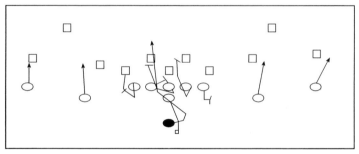

Figure 10-4. Slot Rover—22 X Left

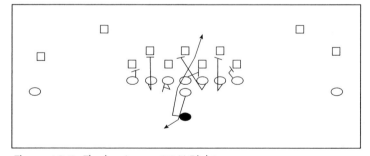

Figure 10-5. Flanker Larry—23 X Right

22 AND 23 OG DRAW

22 and 23 OG Draw is designed to attack an aggressive playside defensive end. The playside offensive tackle sets and punches before he releases inside for the linebacker (Figures 10-6 and 10-7).

Rules for 22 and 23 OG Draw:

PT – Raises up and punches the defensive end. PT then releases inside for the playside linebacker.

PG – Takes a drop step and then base blocks.

C – Blocks back on BG's defender if uncovered. Base blocks if covered.

BG – Releases playside for a deep G block on the playside defensive end.

SE/B/TE – Run defenders off and then stalk block.

MB – Goes in long or extra-long motion to run off and/or stalk block.

F – Raises up and steps to the side called. The fullback waits for the ball and then breaks toward the OG block.

Q – Opens to the side called and gives the ball to the fullback. The quarterback then continues away in the same direction.

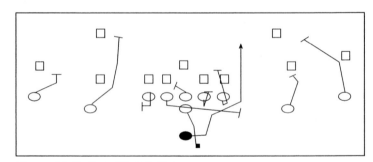

Figure 10-6. Slot—22 OG Right

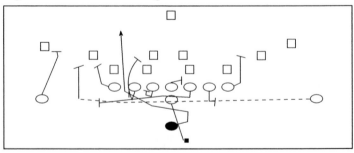

Figure 10-7. Flanker Larry—22 OG Left

GT HITCH

GT Hitch is a hitch screen to the end or back. The playside guard and tackle pull to block (Figures 10-8 and 10-9).

Rules for GT Hitch:

PT and PG – Pull laterally to block for the split end or back.

C – Base blocks if covered, or the first down lineman towards the GT side.

BG and BT – Base block.

E – Takes a step up and two steps back to receive the hitch pass, then reads the PT and PG blocks as he is trying to get outside.

MB – Motions out to E and stalk blocks E's defender.

F – Dives hard to playside to block the second down lineman from the center.

B – Stalk blocks his defender.

Q – Throws to either end depending on who is in better position. The GT side is the primary and the trip side is secondary. This is a presnap decision made at the end of the long motion. Once Q decides where he's throwing, he takes one step back and throws to the spot where E was standing.

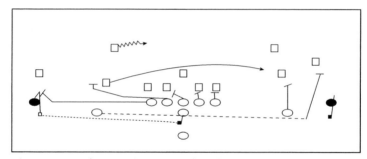

Figure 10-8. Slot Reggie—GT Hitch Left

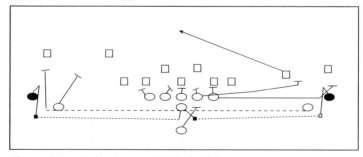

Figure 10-9. Twins Larry—GT Hitch Right

OUTSIDE SCREEN

Outside Screen uses the guards and center to block for the fullback. The tight end screens will call the name of the tight end (Figures 10-10 and 10-11).

Rules for Outside Screen:

Ts – Dropback and then cut their defenders.

Gs and C – Take a drop step and hold for two counts. The three linemen will release laterally for 10 yards before going upfield. These three linemen block areas. The playside guard blocks outside force. The center blocks middle force and the backside guard blocks inside defenders. Linemen can cut block on screens.

B – On playside F screen, he comes hard inside to crack playside linebacker.

MB – Stalk blocks.

SE – Runs off and stalk blocks.

TE (Y) – Pass blocks the defense for two counts on Y screen. TE then releases outside laterally behind the line of scrimmage for 8 yards for the screen pass.

F – On F screen, steps towards the playside tackle and allows him to push defensive end upfield. If the defense has a playside ripper, F blocks this defender for two counts before releasing 8 yards laterally behind the line of scrimmage for the screen.

Q – Drops quickly while looking the defenders off, then loops the ball over to the side called. The screen could be to F or to a specific TE.

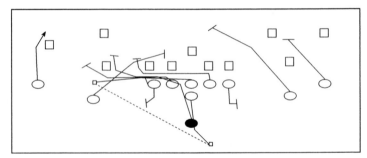

Figure 10-10. Slot–FB Screen Left

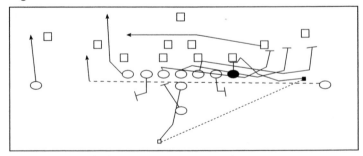

Figure 10-11. Flanker Larry–Y Screen Right

MIDDLE SCREEN

Middle Screen uses the offensive linemen to set up and then block downfield. The middle screen is for the fullback or slot and can be out of the shotgun formation (Figures 10-12 and 10-13).

Rules for Middle Screen:

Gs and C – Take a right set step and block for two counts. Then all three release their defenders to the right side before going upfield for linebackers.

Ts – Run defenders upfield and then check inside for trailers.

Es/MB – Run defenders off and then stalk block.

F – Steps down to the inside hip of the right tackle. F holds for two counts before turning left behind the line of scrimmage where the quarterback stood. On Slot-Middle Screen, F cut blocks the defender aligned on the slot receiving the screen.

B – Runs his defender off and then stalk blocks. On Slot-Middle Screen, the slot takes a step up and then comes laterally to the middle and under the rush.

Q – Comes back quickly about 12 yards and looks defenders off. Q then loops the ball over the middle to the fullback or slot. In Gun, Q takes three to four steps back.

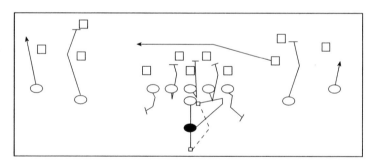

Figure 10-12. Slot–F Middle Screen

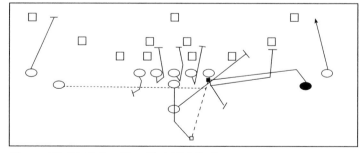

Figure 10-13. Twins Rip–Slot-Middle Screen

SPLIT-END QUICK SCREEN

Split-End Quick Screen is a quick hitting play to the ends (Figures 10-14 and 10-15).

Rules for Split-End Quick Screen:

PT – Releases laterally on snap and blocks force man over the slot.

BT – Runs defender upfield.

PG – Punches and releases to the left for the alley, checking for playside backers.

BG – Takes an inside set step and jabs before releasing left for linebackers and secondary.

C – Takes a quick-drop step and releases left for middle backers.

Playside SE – Takes a quick-jab step and releases inside down the line of scrimmage to where the B was standing. Once ball is caught, gets upfield in the alley.

Backside SE – Stalk blocks.

Playside B – Blocks out on E's defender.

Backside B – Stalk blocks for the F.

F – Runs the scoot route as a secondary read.

Q – Takes two quick steps back and throws directly at the spot the slot was standing. The SE will be at that position to catch the ball. F is Q's secondary read.

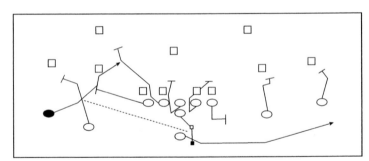

Figure 10-14. Slot X Quick Screen Left vs. Cover 2

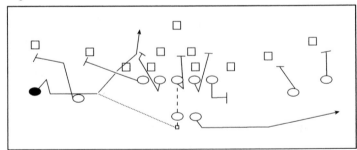

Figure 10-15. Gun–X Screen Left vs. Cover 1

CHAPTER 11

80 Series

The spread option offense has two series (80 and 90) in which all the plays are a Check-With-Me. The 80 Series, or the Goal Line Check-With-Me series, offers flexibility in calling plays in goal-line situations.

When calling these plays, the quarterback's second number is the play. For example, if he calls 44-89, the play is a left toss to the motion man (with short motion) or to the one back (with medium motion). In the wing formation, the quarterback lifts his leg for short motion. As soon as the motion back is near his position, the quarterback snaps the ball. For medium motion, the quarterback pats his hip on the side of the wing he wants to go in motion. This series needs to be quick to catch the defense out of position.

The double wing is the most common formation in the 80 Series. The wing formation places the wingbacks slightly deeper and behind the tight ends. It is almost a Straight T. You want bigger tight ends to help punch the ball in the end zone. In practice, teach the quarterback the areas of weakness in the different goal-line defenses. The quarterback can use four different running plays: Sneak, Lead, Power, or Toss. He also has the option to call the Power Pass.

Plays and numbers for each audible:

- 80 – Power Pass Right
- 81 – Power Pass Left
- 82 through 85 – Lead
- 86/87 – Power
- 88/89 – Zone Toss

If the quarterback wants to call the sneak, he just scratches the butt of the center and pulls up his hands for the silent snap. On every 80 Series play, the offensive line needs to first check for the sneak. If the quarterback does not have down linemen in the A gaps, he can call for the silent sneak when he only needs one or two yards.

The rest of this chapter examines different goal line defenses and their weaknesses against the double-wing formation. You can call other plays out of the double wing, but this chapter will focus only on the 80 Series. These plays can use the fullback or tailback deep, and the motion can be short or medium.

LEAD CHECK-WITH-ME

If the A or B gap has an opening, the lead may be an excellent choice. If the defense is a 6-2 Goal Line, the B gaps are good areas to attack. This is a double lead by the backs (Figures 11-1 and 11-2).

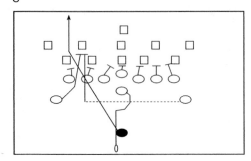

Figure 11-1. 14-82, 14-82

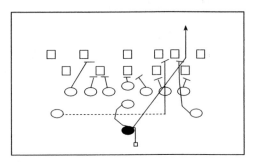

Figure 11-2. 30-83, 30-83

When the defense is playing a 5-3 Stack Goal Line, run in the C gaps, as shown in Figures 11-3 and 11-4.

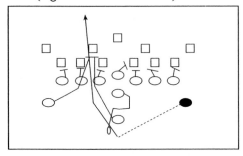

Figure 11-3. 14-85, 14-85

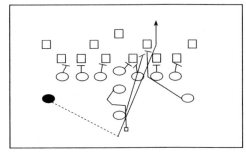

Figure 11-4. 58-84, 58-84

POWER CHECK-WITH-ME

The power is an excellent play versus a 6-5 Goal Line. Power is also good against any goal-line defense where the defensive end is wide (Figures 11-5 and 11-6).

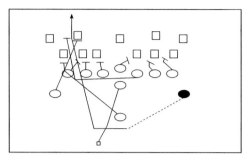

Figure 11-5. 18-87, 18-87

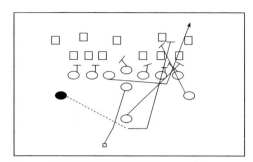

Figure 11-6. 67-86, 67-86

Against a Gap 8 defense, the playside wing needs to come inside and combo block with the tight end and seal on linebackers. The backside tackle may have to reach block for the pulling OG (Figures 11-7 and 11-8).

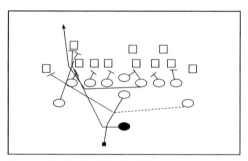

Figure 11-7. 15-87, 15-87

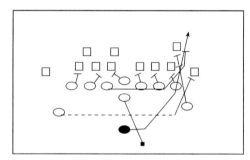

Figure 11-8. 31-86, 31-86

TOSS CHECK-WITH-ME

The toss can be effective any time your opponent lines up with only one defender on the outside. When you're facing two or three players outside, the quarterback needs to check to an inside play. The wingback must make a decision whether to block down or out. If he sees a wide 9 technique, the wing should block down. If the defensive end is inside or head-up, the wing can block force him outside. The wing can also cheat the outside alignment on toss. 88 and 89 are the two-toss audibles (Figures 11-9 through 11-12).

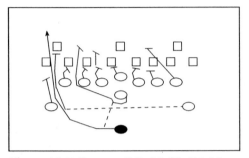

Figure 11-9. Toss vs. 6-2. 54-89, 54-89

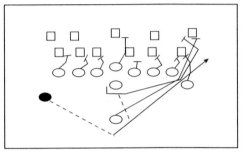

Figure 11-10. Toss vs. 6-5. 22-88, 22-88

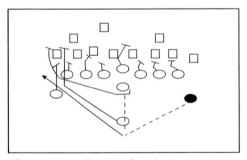

Figure 11-11. Toss vs. Gap 8. 99-89, 99-89

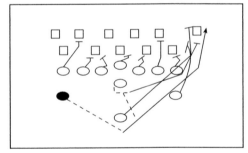

Figure 11-12. Toss vs. 5-3 Stack. 10-88, 10-88

POWER PASS

The Power Pass is a good goal-line play-action pass. The tight ends release inside as if to block, the quarterback gets away from the line of scrimmage, and the fullback places a lot of pressure on the outside linebacker to step up and stop the run.

If the quarterback feels everyone is on the line of scrimmage and playing run, he can call 80 (right) or 81 (left) (Figure 11-13).

Rules for Power Pass:

PT – Aggressively blocks down with the PTE, but stays on the line of scrimmage.

BT – Down blocks any defender in the B gap if BG and C are covered.

PG – Aggressively blocks down, but stays on the line of scrimmage, unless Q yells "Go."

BG – OG blocks playside for the quarterback.

C – Blocks down and stays on the line of scrimmage.

PTE – Down blocks with the PT. The playside tackle then releases up on a 4 route climbing to the back corner of the end zone.

BTE – Down blocks hard, then releases in the back of the end zone between the goal posts.

W – Comes inside and down blocks the defensive end, but plants and runs a 2 route inside the goal line.

F or load blocker – Comes hard downhill and chips the first defender outside the defensive end, then releases in the flat along the goal line.

MB or ball carrier – Comes lateral 90 degrees over the playside tackle. MB then cuts hard downhill on the fake and blocks the first defender over the end that shows.

Q – Opens deep at a 45-degree angle and fakes to MB. Q can read levels, or the second secondary defender, as his position read. The position read is for PTE or wing. The secondary read is the fullback's flat or BTE under the goal posts.

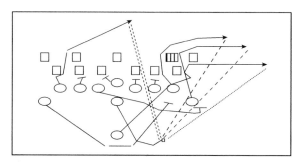

Figure 11-13. 46-80, 46-80

CHAPTER 12

90 Series

The 90 Series is a Check-With-Me on the line of scrimmage. The formation is usually slot or twins, but could also be flanker or wing. The quarterback should read the box and count 0-1-2.

If you are playing a team with multiple defensive fronts, the 90 Series allows you to make a good call. The running plays in the 90 Series are draw (92/93), inside veer (94/95), and speed option (98/99). The passes are Quick 01 (90), Quick 10 (91), Stop 68 (96), and Stop 74 (97).

In the huddle the quarterback calls, "90 Check-with-me." When he comes to the line of scrimmage, he yells "down," then two different numbers. The second digit number is the play. So if he yells, "Down, 48-91, 48-91," the play is a Quick-10 pass.

These audibles can be run with short, medium, and long motions. The quarterback just turns to the back on that side and lifts his leg for short motion, or pats his hip for medium and long motions. On the long and medium motions, the motion backs and second receiver must learn all the combination routes for these audibles. If the quarterback calls for a short motion, he can still pass the ball with maximum protection. From week to week, you should cover the blocking schemes in practice.

Even after motion has begun, the quarterback can still change his audible because the defense may have jumped into a different alignment. To do this, the quarterback yells, "Check, check," and gives another set of numbers.

QUICK PASSES IN THE 90 SERIES (90 - 91)

Slot—14-90, 14-90 (Figure 12-1)

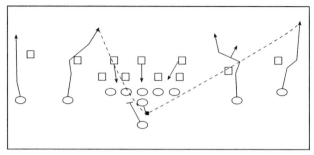

Figure 12-1. Slot—14-90, 14-90

Twins—42-91, 42-91 (Figure 12-2)

To call 91 Check, the twins need to be wide. This combination uses a presnap read. The wide receiver on the left goes under the pick. When the secondary is playing a loose zero, the coverage is attacked in the flats and deep middle. If the quarterback notes the cornerback jumping on the 1 route, he can throw deep to the 0 route.

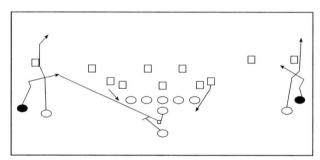

Figure 12-2. Twins—42-91, 42-91

Slot—19-91, 19-91 (Figure 12-3)

If the quarterback puts the motion man in medium motion on 91 Check, the motion man runs a skinny 7 route, but looks for the ball quickly in the seam and alley. This progression read tells the quarterback the backside 1 route and frontside 0 route are *hot* and his primary receiver is the frontside 1 route. The motion man runs a 7 route and is the second read, but cannot allow the playside linebacker to come underneath for the interception.

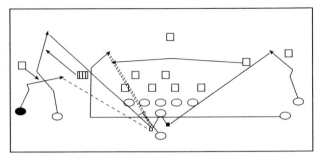

Figure 12-3. Slot—19-91, 19-91

DRAWS IN THE 90 SERIES (92 - 93)

Slot—76-93, 76-93 (Figure 12-4)

The offense could game plan to run the 92 Check with a backside X block because the draw is an excellent play versus cover 2.

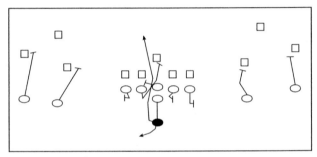

Figure 12-4. Slot – 76-93, 76-93

Slot—19-92, 19-92 (Figure 12-5)

On motion that doesn't affect the blocking, the motion back can go as far as he wants to distract the defense.

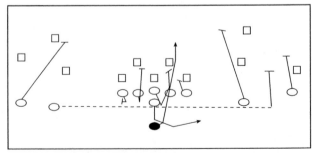

Figure 12-5. Slot—19-92, 19-92

INSIDE VEER IN THE 90 SERIES (94 - 95)

The go-to play in the 90 Series is the inside veer, which you can run with short or medium motion. It works best against 1 or 2 coverage. The quarterback can give, keep, or run.

The key to this play is the block of the playside guard. He must not allow penetration by a 2 or 3 technique.

Slot–23-94, 23-94 (Figure 12-6)

Against the 50/noseguard, run the inside veer at the bubble and away from the nose shade if possible. If he is on the left shade of the center, run 94. If he is on the right side of the center, run 95. If the playside guard believes the nose will be blocked, he can go to the playside linebacker, or down on the backside linebacker.

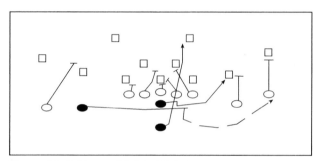

Figure 12-6. Slot – 23-94, 23-94

Slot–31-95, 31-95 (Figure 12-7)

If the defense is giving up an inside running lane or shifting towards the motion, the quarterback can still run the inside and speed-option weakside.

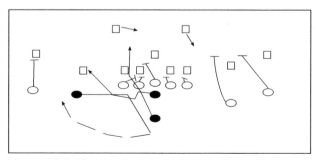

Figure 12-7. Slot–31-95, 31-95

STOP PASSES IN THE 90 SERIES (96 - 97)

In the two-stop passes, the quarterback must be careful not to throw an interception or get sacked. He must not throw into a double coverage or get sacked from an extra defender in the box. If he sees seven rushers versus the slot formation, the quarterback can use short motion to keep a second back in for maximum protection. Or, he can change the play to a quick pass. If he feels any pressure, the quarterback should throw the ball into the stands. On the 96 Check, the outside receiver will run an out route for the five-step drop. When the cornerback plays the outside receiver tight, the receiver should pretend to run the fade, but break it back at 12 yards deep. The second receiver runs a normal 8 route.

Slot—32-96, 32-96 (Figure 12-8)

When the free safety is up playing run, 96 Check could have success. The quarterback gets a strong presnap read. He takes his drop and makes his position read. If the cornerback drops back quickly into his third, the quarterback throws over the outside linebacker/strong safety to the outside receiver's short comeback. If the corner sits on the short comeback, the quarterback throws deep to the 8 route.

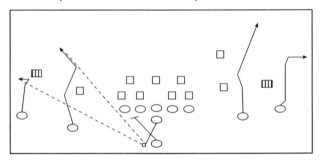

Figure 12-8. Slot—32-96, 32-96

Slot—14-96, 14-96 (Figure 12-9)

Because the stop pass is a five-step drop back, the quarterback may need an extra blocker on the backside versus zero coverage, and he can use short motion. This tells the motion back to block to the strongside as the fullback blocks weakside for maximum protection. The backside receiver runs the read route.

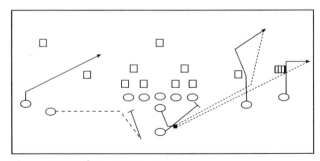

Figure 12-9. Slot—14-96, 14-96

Slot–28-97, 28-97 (Figure 12-10)

The 97 Check can be a big payday when the defense does not have a defender deep in the middle and the linebackers are playing off the line of scrimmage. The 97 Check attacks the deep middle and flats. If the quarterback has time, the 7 route could score. This pass is also good against a cover 1. In a 1 coverage, the second receiver must set up the defender for the outside pick.

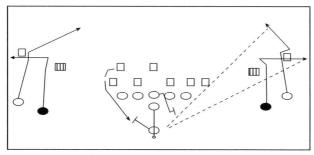

Figure 12-10. Slot –28-97, 28-97

SPEED OPTION IN THE 90 SERIES (98 -99)

Speed option is the last play in the 90 Series. This is a weakside and no-motion running play. You can run it to the motion side, but then you will need to block more defenders. You can even call 98/99 Check against a blitzing-zero coverage. If more than one defender is positioned to the outside of the playside tackle, the playside tackle must not allow both defenders to cross the line of scrimmage. The playside tackle must reach block the defender covering his position, or the quarterback must change the play.

Slot–77-98, 77-98 (Figure 12-11)

Besides throwing the backside-read route, the quarterback may attack the weakside with the speed option because the secondary is in a man coverage. This occurs when a defender runs across the formation to the strongside, also known as the unwelcome stranger. For example, if the quarterback called a 91 Check with long motion and the backside defender ran across the formation, the quarterback could still change the play to a 99 Check.

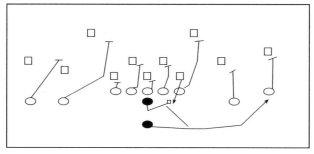

Figure 12-11. Slot–77-98, 77-98

Slot—54-99, 54-99 (Figure 12-12)

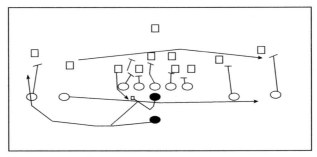

Figure 12-12. Slot—54-99, 54-99

SUMMARY

The 90 Series is excellent for an intelligent quarterback who will take charge and make things happen. The draw, inside veer, speed option, and a couple of quick and stop passes will be all the audibles needed during the season. If your offense perfects these combinations out of different formations and motion, the quarterback should always have an opportunity for a great play.

CHAPTER 13

Special Plays

Trick plays can be very good, or very bad, but every offense should know a couple of special plays. These special, or trick plays, are important because they promote excitement among the players, and they tend to keep the defense honest. If the defense knows about your special plays, they usually have to take time away from their regular practice to prepare for those plays.

The spread option offense uses the following five trick plays: double pass, reverse off the fullback toss, tailback pass off the toss action, fullback reverse pass, and wraparound. Special/trick plays are risky, but they are fun and can break a game open!

DOUBLE PASS

The double pass has four key steps (Figure 13-1):

1. The quarterback throws a long lateral pass to a split end.

2. The split end catches the ball.

3. The split end throws a deep pass to the slot, and

4. the slot catches the ball.

The double pass uses a double-slot formation and Larry motion if the split end is right-handed. A right-handed split end is in a better position to throw the second pass from the left side. The double pass works best when the safeties are coming hard on support.

Rules for Double Pass:

Offensive Line – Uses aggressive pass blocking.

PE – Takes a step up and then four steps back for his backwards pass. After catching the pass, PE then throws a deep pass to the slot running the 8 route.

MB – Goes into long motion next to PE, then steps up and blocks the first threat to PE.

B – Releases towards his defender and slows up as if to block him, then releases outside and runs the 8 route. B receives the pass from the playside end.

F – Swings out the opposite direction of the double pass. If the secondary is playing tight and not allowing the double pass, the fullback must be ready for the swing pass. F is the second option.

BE – Runs a read route in case the PE is covered.

Q – Checks the secondary's reaction to motion. If the cornerback is off PE by at least 5 yards, Q turns and throws a backward pass to PE. If the coverage is tight, the Q turns to BE running a slant or fade, or the F running a swing route.

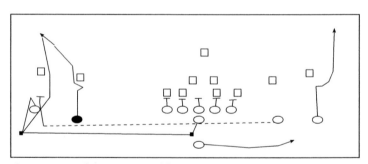

Figure 13-1. Slot Larry—Double Pass

REVERSE OFF THE FULLBACK TOSS

In a reverse off the fullback toss, the fullback catches the toss and hands it off to the back coming around for the reverse (Figure 13-2). This reverse is not difficult to execute, but the offensive line must not allow the defensive line to penetrate deep past the line of scrimmage. For the reverse to have success, the defense must be attacking the direction of the play. Also, the backside defensive end and tackle must not push the reverse too deep.

This play works best in a double-flanker formation. The play uses the fullback toss for the reverse because it does not push the reverse man too deep.

Rules for Reverse Off the Fullback Toss:

Offensive Line – Zone steps to the toss side and locks on to their defenders. Must not allow penetration. The backside tackle can use a wheel block only if his defender doesn't penetrate upfield.

PE – Zone blocks playside and locks on to the defender. The playside tight end can use the wheel block by stepping in front of the defensive end and looping around for a blind-side block.

F – Receives the toss and hands the ball to reverse man off his outside hip.

B – Reverses back to the middle to receive the handoff from the fullback. B tries to get to the outside following the block of the quarterback.

Q – Reverses out and tosses to the fullback. The quarterback then breaks back the opposite direction to lead block on the cornerback.

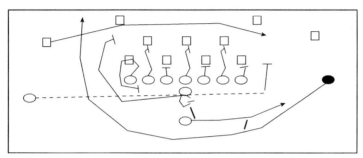

Figure 13-2. Flanker Reggie—28 Reverse

TAILBACK PASS

The tailback pass is a great play against cornerbacks that play the run. The quarterback tosses to the motion man in short motion as the offensive line zone blocks playside without going downfield. After the tailback sells the run, he throws deep to the flanker or end. For this play to succeed, the playside cornerback must bite on the flow of the toss action. The tailback must be able to throw the ball accurately at least 30 yards. This play can use a double-flanker or double-slot formation (Figure 13-3).

Rules for Tailback Pass:

Offensive Line – Zone blocks playside and stays on the line of scrimmage.

TEs – Stay on the line of scrimmage and block as if the play was a toss.

B – Releases upfield as if to block the cornerback when he is the slot. As the flanker receiver, he slows down as if to block the corner, then releases to the outside on a fade.

F – Releases playside and blocks force man.

MB/T – Goes in short motion. The tailback receives the toss and breaks to the sideline as if the play was a toss. He then throws a deep pass to the flanker.

Q – Reverses out and tosses to the tailback, motion man. Q then helps block playside as if it was a toss.

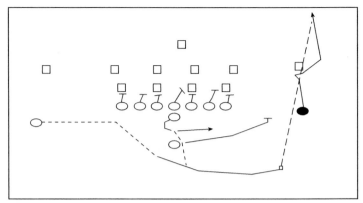

Figure 13-3. Flanker Roy—48 TB Pass

REVERSE PASS

The 48 reverse pass uses a double-flanker formation. This play is one of the hardest trick plays because it takes so long to develop and the defense must stay at home for it to succeed. This play can also be 28 Reverse Pass.

The reverse pass has five steps (Figure 13-4):

1. The quarterback makes a good pitch to the motion back.

2. The back makes a good handoff to the slot.

3. The slot tosses the ball back to the quarterback.

4. The quarterback throws a deep pass to the fullback running down the sideline.

5. Finally, the back catches the ball. This must all happen without the quarterback getting sacked.

Rules for Reverse Pass:

Offensive Line – Zone blocks to the right and locks on to their defenders. The offensive line must not allow penetration. Uncovered linemen can zone playside and help double, but they must check for aggressive linebackers.

TEs – Zone block playside. TEs must not allow defensive ends upfield.

F – Releases wide as if to block force, then releases outside and runs a fade.

MB – Takes the toss from the quarterback and releases wide, but hands off to the back, who is coming around for the reverse. The fullback then blocks any defenders trailing the play.

B – Reverses back for the handoff from the back. As soon as the back receives the handoff, he tosses to the quarterback. The back then helps block.

Q – Reverses out and tosses to the back. The quarterback releases back at a 45-degree angle towards the playside. Once the ball comes back on the reverse, the back flips the ball to the quarterback, who throws deep to the motion fullback on the fade.

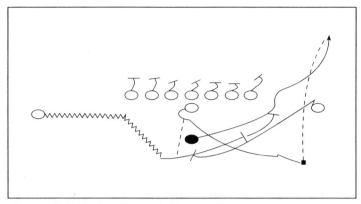

Figure 13-4. Flanker Roy—48 Reverse Pass

WRAPAROUND

Wraparound is a special running play that attacks a swarming defense. The quarterback reverses and sprints to the sideline. As he passes behind the wingback, he slips the ball under the wingback's arm. The objective is to get the defense to overreact and run past the wingback holding the ball. The key to this play is the exchange from the quarterback to the wingback (Figure 13-5).

Rules for Wraparound:

Offensive Line and TEs – Zone block to the right.

Wing – Slides one step to the left and turns slightly towards the playside tight end while raising his right elbow. The wing slumps over to form a pocket. The quarterback will come around from behind and slip the ball into the back of the wing's right side. After the handoff, the wingback must count, "One thousand one, one thousand two, one thousand three" before cutting back to the left behind the pursuit.

F – Releases laterally around the wingback next to his right side to help shield the view of the handoff.

Q – Reverses out and runs laterally behind the wing while following the fullback off-tackle. As he reverses out, the quarterback uses his left hand to slip the ball under the wing's right arm. The quarterback then continues on to the sideline as if he has the ball.

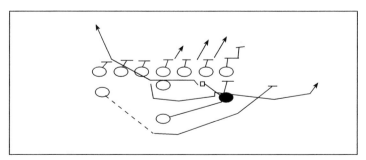

Figure 13-5. Wing Roy—Wrap

CHAPTER 14

Practices and Organization

The length of a team's offensive workout depends on its size and program. A team that uses a two-platoon system can spend a lot of time practicing its offensive plays. Smaller teams that use the same players on offense, defense, and the kicking game will spend less practice time on offense because they have to divide their workouts.

Regardless of how long you practice, you should focus on teaching the proper fundamentals, techniques, and execution. Never assume a player has prior knowledge of a fundamental, technique, or anything else about a position. Do not allow a player to execute a fundamental incorrectly. Through drills, you should map out every technique and step to improve each player's execution. Explain each fundamental from the first step through the entire process, and make sure the player understands all the terminology used. Coach on the run and give players instruction as they are doing the fundamentals. Take your time teaching at the beginning of the season. In the long run, it will save time because you will not have to review basic fundamentals over and over again.

TWO PLATOON

If your team uses a two-platoon system, your offense will have a greater amount of time to develop its skills and timing for execution. Your team's play selection should contain many of the plays discussed in this book. In a two-platoon system, the players will have more individual and group-practice time. The offensive teams (Varsity and JV) learn their fundamentals and timing during these workouts. When the offense and defense break into the team segment of practice, the JV defense becomes the scout team for the Varsity offense, and the JV offense becomes the scout team for the Varsity defense.

IRON MAN

If your team doesn't have the athletes or numbers to two platoon, you will have to break practices into offense, defense, and special teams. You should decide how much time to spend on offense, usually at least one hour each day. You should limit your play list to what you feel will be most effective.

A team with small numbers may have to practice half-lines or go against air, which is not always bad. In these situations, you can work on cadence, timing, certain small techniques, and audibles.

INDIVIDUAL

If you have enough time and enough coaches, divide your practice into individual, group, and team workouts. Devote the first 10 or 15 minutes of practice to working on individual fundamentals. During this time, players should work on drills or techniques specific to their positions.

The offensive line coach should begin with the proper position of the three-point stance. He shows players how to distribute their weight on their feet, and how to position their backs and necks. Then, he uses a drill to start the linemen from their stance. During this time, the offensive line coach drills 1-on-1 blocking, combos, doubles, zones, downs, G's, heel-toes, and any other blocks used in the offense. The boards, sled, and chutes are excellent tools for teaching and conditioning linemen.

The quarterbacks should do specific drills that deal with movement, option, drops, and steps. They can also work routes with receivers against air, play timing, cones and releases, breaks and deliveries, and any other drill that will improve execution.

The backs can work on first steps, pocket position, blocking, handoff lines, ball drills, cones and plants, and catching drills. They should also practice play timing on running plays with the quarterback and routes.

Receivers can work on releases and breaks. The hand position, eyes, tucks, and shoulder drills are excellent with the stalk techniques. Routes against air, breaks and delivery, picks, and reads are done with quarterbacks and other receivers.

You should always reinforce individual techniques during all segments of practice. However, the individual segment of practice gives you quality teaching time and helps ensure that players understand what you are teaching.

GROUP

Group phases of practice are important because they give players the opportunity to run plays over and over, thereby improving their fundamentals and execution. Use group practice time to work plays that don't require all the personnel from each side of the ball. In a group workout, the offense and defense divide into *hulls*. The inside hull, for example, consists of the members of the box. The offense works running plays inside the tackles. The outside hull consists of ends, outside linebackers, and secondary. The option drill can use half lines. 7-on-7 should use receivers, backs, secondary, and linebackers together to work on the passing game. You should script the plays that they run in group work.

TEAM

The team phase of practice is the most important. If you only have 30 minutes a day to practice offense, spend that time in team workouts. Always script the team segment of practice. If numbers permit, two offensive teams should alternate against a scout team.

Remember: you need to coach on the run. Don't waste time standing around waiting for a player. Go meet that player after the play and jog back to the huddle while giving feedback. If you have a number of players standing around during team, you probably need to revise the structure of practice to involve more players.

The JV team should act as the scout team for the Varsity. The JV defense should have a coach aligning them according to the script sheet. Before the Varsity offense runs a play, the head coach and/or offensive coordinator will declare the tackle mode (red for no tackle; green for tackle). The offensive team must give 100 percent on each play for all modes.

If you have enough players, the offense can form a second team and alternate against the JV defense. But in order to have two offensive huddles, the JV defense must have backups to provide for breaks. The two offensive groups will pound the JV. As one team completes a play, the next team breaks the huddle.

You can divide team practice time into just running or passing. Or, to make practice more game-like, you can combine the two.

FIVE-MINUTE PERIODS

Break up each practice into five-minute periods. This helps you stay on schedule and prevents you from spending too much time on a drill, a fundamental, or a play. A student trainer with 20 four-inch numbers signals the period every five minutes. The trainer blows a whistle or horn to signal the beginning of each period.

TWO-HOUR LIMIT

Practice should not last more than two hours. Players and coaches tend to lose concentration and endurance after that time. Some situations require longer practices, but as a whole, keeping players fresh for games is more important than practicing 15 extra minutes. If you can't get all of your offense and fundamental work done in two hours, you probably have way too much offense.

If you have athletics in the first morning hour, you can practice the team before school for an hour and forty-five minutes. Then the players and coaches can come back after school and repeat the same practice. But practicing twice a day all season long can wear out your players and lead to burnout.

INSTALLATION SHEET

The offensive coordinator needs to have a play-installation sheet at the beginning of and during the season. At the beginning of two-a-day workouts, the offensive coordinator should list the plays and series he wants in place by a certain date. These dates may change, but you need to start with a definite plan of attack. Installation sheets help you monitor the progress of the offense and keep coaches organized. Figure 14-1 illustrates an example of a beginning installation sheet.   You   should decide what plays need to go in first based on personnel. The 90 Series is a great way to start. The 90 Check Series will motivate the quarterback at the very beginning because it has the option and the basis of the passing attack. Be aggressive and never feel that the players cannot execute this offense.

Spread Offense Installation Sheet

Week 1	Formation	Motion	Plays	Audibles
Day 1 A.M.	Slot/Flanker	Roy/Lou	14/15 In	
	Slot/Flanker	Reg/Lat	18/19 Speed	
	Slot/Flanker	Reg/Lar	20/21 Trap	
	Slot/Flanker	Roy/Lou	1-14/15-74	
	Slot/Flanker	None	Quick 10/01	
Day 1 P.M.	Wing/Twins	Roy/Lou	Lead Check	
	Wing/Twins	Roy/Lou	46/47 Counter	
	Wing/Twins	Roy/Lou	46/47 Bootleg	
	Wing/Twins	Roy/Lou	48/49 Zone	
Day 2 A.M.	Review all plays from Day 1, but in opposite formations.			
Day 2 P.M.	Slot/Flanker	Roy/Lou	10/11 Mid	
	Slot/Flanker	Roy/Lou	14/15 OG	
	Slot/Flanker	Reg/Lar	Quick 072	
	Slot/Flanker	Rip/Lip	Quick 107	

Week 1	Formation	Motion	Plays	Audibles
Day 3 A.M.	Review all plays from Days 1 and 2.			
Day 3 P.M.	Slot	Roy/Lou/Lar/Reg Rip/Lip		90 Checks
Day 4 A.M.	Scrimmage using all plays.			
Day 4 P.M.	Slot/Flanker	Roy/Lou	14/15 X	Lead Check
	Slot/Flanker	Rover/Lass	Stop 48	Quick Check
	Slot/Flanker	Roy/Lou	46/47 Power	

Figure 14-1. Spread Offense Installation Sheet

CHAPTER 15

Strategy and Talent

The spread option offense is just one of many productive offenses. The bottom line is that you have to know your players' strengths and decide how to use them in a game. The game plan is extremely important, but not as important as the abilities of the players running the plays. You must develop the team's strategy according to the offensive personnel.

Calling plays in a game is very difficult. You have a hundred items to consider when making a decision, but just a few seconds to make the call. The following tips can help you plan your strategy before and during a game:

- If you have a great running attack or passing attack, stay with it until you are stopped. If your offense is not really outstanding in either passing or running, you need to run and pass just to leave a question in the defenders' minds. That question can be all the hesitation you need to score.

- Be patient in running. If your opponent has an outstanding offense, take some time off the clock and run the ball. Running sets up the big play-action pass.

- On first down plays, stay with quicks, stops, and play-action passes. You want to avoid second and long, or third and long situations.

- Use screens on second and long situations, but not on third and long.

- On third and long plays, always pass the ball past the first-down markers

- Do not call a bootleg in passing situations, unless you are using it as roll protection and you have a back to cut block the ripper.

- Play-action passes work best after you've had success running the ball.

- If you can't run against five in the box, try the double-flanker and wing formations for extra people and better angles.

- Save the fan passes for third downs to stay out of third and extra-long situations.

- Pay attention to how the defense reacts to motion, what types of slants and pinches the defense runs, and who comes on the blitzes. Keep these factors in mind when choosing plays.

- When setting up plays, wait a couple of plays or a quarter. The defender is not stupid.

- Don't use a trick play on long situations.

- Remember that when you're inside the 50-yard line, you are in four-down territory, so you still have an extra down to run the ball.

- Stay on your game plan. Remember, if you are two touchdowns behind in the fourth quarter, you still have a chance to come back. If you are three touchdowns behind in the fourth quarter, it becomes very difficult to even the score.

The coach calling the plays must have a great understanding of the 0-1-2 rule. This book has discussed many different types of defenses and how they should be attacked. The next section contains a base call sheet and a down-and-distance call sheet. The one drawback to the spread option is the coordinator must be ready for any type of defense given. Many times defensive coordinators will change their normal defense to defend the spread option.

BASE CALL SHEET

The preliminary game plan is laid out in a base call sheet. The base call sheet shows all the plays that would be effective against cover zero, cover 1, and cover 2, and against no motion, man, or zone in each coverage. It classifies the plays by formation (slot/twins and flanker/wing) and type of play (running or passing). See Figure 15-1 for an example of a base call sheet.

Running Plays vs. Cover Zero

Slot/Twins vs. No motion	*Slot/Twins vs. man*	*Slot/Twins vs. zone*
20/21 Trap	19/18 Weak	SL Roy/Lou 14/15
12/13 Base	46/47 Counter Weak	Roy/Lou Power

Flanker/Wing vs. No motion	*Flanker/Wing vs. man*	*Flanker/Wing vs. zone*
18/19 zone	Roy/Lou 14/15	Roy/Lou Lead Check
26/27 Counter	Roy/Lou 14/15 OG St.	Rip/Lip 68/69 Toss

Passing Plays vs. Cover Zero

Slot/Twins vs. No motion	*Slot/Twins vs. man*	*Slot/Twins vs. zone*
Q-01/10	Q-872	Q-107
E Double Screen	Roy/Lou Stop 9S	Q-Rip/Lip Boot Strong

Flanker/Wing vs. No motion	*Flanker/Wing vs. man*	*Flanker/Wing vs. zone*
26/27 Boot	Rip/Lip Q-027	Roy/Lou Power Pass
Stop-7B	Roy/Lou Lead Pass	46/47 Boot

Running Plays vs. Cover 1

Slot/Twins vs. No motion	*Slot/Twins vs. man*	*Slot/Twins vs. zone*
18/19 Speed	Reg/Lar Counter Weak	Roy/Lou 14/15 In
14/15 X	Reg/Lar 18/19 Weak	Rip/Lou 14/15 Belly

Flanker/Wing vs. No motion	*Flanker/Wing vs. man*	*Flanker/Wing vs. zone*
20/21 Trap	Rip/Lip 66/67 Power	Roy/Lou 14/15 In
64/65 Counter	Roy/Lou 14/15 G	Reg/Lar 64/65 zone

Passing Plays vs. Cover 1

Slot/Twins vs. No motion	*Slot/Twins vs. man*	*Slot/Twins vs. zone*
Stop 48/74	Roy/Lou 1-14/15-48/74	Rov/Las Stop-872
Stop 53-48 Scat	Reg/Lar Boot Weak Bench	Rip/Lip 66/67 Boot Strong

Flanker/Wing vs. No motion	*Flanker/Wing vs. man*	*Flanker/Wing vs. zone*
Stop - 68	Roy/Lou Lead Pass	Rov/Lar Stop
Stop - 48/5D Scoot	Reg/Lar TE Screen Weaks	Roy 1-14 Dump

Running Plays vs. Cover 2

Slot/Twins vs. No motion	*Slot/Twins vs. man*	*Slot/Twins vs. zone*
20/21 Trap	Roy/Lou 46/47 Power	Roy/Lou 14/15 In
22/23 X Draw	Rip/Lip 26/27 Counter Weak	Rip/Lip 28/29 GOG

Flanker/Wing vs. No motion	*Flanker/Wing vs. man*	*Flanker/Wing vs. zone*
14/15 G Keep	Roy/Lou Lead Check	Reg/Lar Trap Check
64/65 Zone	Roy/Lou 16 Load	Reg/Lar 14/15 In

Passing Plays vs. Cover 2

Slot/Twins vs. No motion	*Slot/Twins vs. man*	*Slot/Twins vs. zone*
Fan - 9S	Reg/Lar Q-107 Dump	Rov/Las Stop 872
Fan - 68 Angle	Rip/Lip Stop 559	Reg/Lar Fan 68C

Flanker/Wing vs. No motion	*Flanker/Wing vs. man*	*Flanker/Wing vs. zone*
26/27 Boot	Rov/Las Q-259	Roy/Lou Power Pass
Q-10	Reg/Lar Stop 74D	Roy/Lou 46/47 BT Stop

Figure 15-1. Base call sheet

DOWN-AND-DISTANCE CALL SHEET

The second call sheet you'll need is a down-and-distance call sheet, which breaks down plays by field zones. When formulating the down-and-distance call sheet, take into account personnel matchups, as well as how you expect the defense to align and react. If the defense behaves differently than you predicted, you can revert to your base call sheet. Figure 15-2 illustrates a down-and-distance sheet with two plays per field zone.

End Zone to -10 yards

1st & 10	2nd & Long	2nd & Med/Short	3rd & Long	3rd & Med	3rd & Short
14/15 In	Q-107	14/15 OG	S-483	1-14/15-74	Lead
18/19 Sp	Outside Scr	10/11Mid	F-9S	Q-BBF	Power

-11 yards to 50 yards

1st & 10	2nd & Long	2nd & Med/Short	3rd & Long	3rd & Med	3rd & Short
90 Check	14/15 X	14/15 G	Fan 784	Q-250	GL CK
1-16/17-7FL	Mid Screen	Toss	G-Boot	Power	69/68

+49 yards to +30 yards

1st & 10	2nd & Long	2nd & Med/Short	3rd & Long	3rd & Med	3rd/4th & Short
46/47 Counter	S-550	26/27 Boot	S-74D	68/69 Counter	GL/CK
GT Hitch	90 CK	28 Rev	Stop CK	18/19 Sp	90 CK

+29 yards to +10 yards

1st & 10	2nd & Long	2nd & Med/Short	3rd & Long	3rd & Med	3rd/4th & Short
Lead Pass	42 Lead Draw	14/15 In	S-74	Q-107	GL/CK
16/17 Load	QK Screen	1-14/15-48	F-68C	90 CK	18/19 zone

+9 yards to + 5 yards

1st & 10	2nd & Long	2nd & Med/Short	3rd & Long	3rd & Med	3rd/4th & Short
14/15 Belly	90 CK	Lead CK	F-86C	90 CK	GL CK
18/19 zone	Q-CK	Boot Strong	S- 5D/48 Scat Q	07	10/11 Mid

+4 yards to End Zone

1st & 10	2nd & Long	2nd & Med/Short	3rd & Med	3rd/4th & Short
1-14 Dump	Q-872	GL CK	1-16 7FL	GL CK
In CK	S-48 Delay	66/67 Boot	Power Pass	GL CK

Figure 15-2. Down-and-distance call sheet

SCRIPTING PLAYS

Having a set of plays to run in the beginning of the game is a good idea. The offensive coordinator should plan plays with certain formations and motion to see how the defense reacts to each. Throughout the game, the defense will use different schemes and make adjustments, but testing their reactions early will give you a good idea of what plays to call later in the game.

80'S AND 90'S

Whenever you are hesitant about calling a play, you can fall back on the 80 and 90 Series. These checks will keep the offense from missing a step, as long as you have done a good job teaching these audibles.

MOTIVATION

Motivation is a great teaching tool. It helps players concentrate through periods of exhaustion and play beyond their ability. You should motivate players with a combination of positive and negative feedback. Remember that most players are smart. They know a *snow job* when they hear one. Time your motivation for when it really counts because players will tune you out after a few minutes.

Many successful programs have used different types of motivation, but the best motivation is competition. When a player believes he can lose his position to another athlete, he will improve faster. Therefore, you should focus on bringing more players into the program to improve the level of competition within your team.

At times players rise to the occasion during a contest in response to a pep talk, but if the pep talk is going to help, you must first motivate your players to learn and master the proper fundamentals.

TALENT

Like any offense, the spread option offense won't work with an untalented group of athletes. A coach may make mistakes in teaching, organization, and even strategy, but he must play the best players available at each position.

When selecting personnel, remember first to consider the defense. Except for the positions of quarterback and fullback, put the most athletic players on defense, not offense. Each position has unique qualities, as discussed in the Introduction. Consider the following requirements carefully when assigning players to positions.

Center

The center must be a smart individual who can make correct line calls on the line of scrimmage. On each play, he must call out if the front is a 40, 50, or Split. He should be consistent with the snap and be able to handle the potential blitz. He needs to have quick feet so he can check frontside on passes and be able to block back. The center should have the concentration level to deal with any audible and Check-With-Me.

Guard

The guard should be the strongest lineman and be able to block a 2 and possibly 3 technique for the inside veer. If he can block a 2 technique, this allows the tackle to base block or come inside to block. This is very important for the offense. He should also be quick enough to pull on G's, Counters, OG's, and Screens. The guard should have the concentration to handle any audible and Check-With-Me. For pass protection, the guard needs good balance and enough strength to handle a bull rush. The guard is your best lineman.

Tackle

The tackle needs to have good feet. If your team is going to run the inside option, the tackle must be able to rip inside and also combo block with the guard. On passes, the tackle must have the feet and balance to deal with quick defensive ends that get upfield and around on the pass rush. The tackle must also have the concentration to deal with any audible and Check-With-Me. Of the three linemen positions (center, guard, and tackle), the tackle is number three on the list of importance.

End

The end should have the characteristics of a basketball player. The end must be strong enough to hook block a defensive end, quick enough to stalk in the open field, and tough enough to go across the middle on a pass.

Good hands are the most important quality needed at this position. Speed is also desirable, but not at the expense of pass-catching ability. The end is a versatile position. He must be able to split out and come in tight. He can be a linebacker type or even a skinny offensive tackle with good feet. This is the one position that you will substitute for during a game. In slot, use a smaller player if needed. In flanker, use the traditional tight-end type.

The end also must have a high concentration level to execute any audible or Check-With-Me in a game. He must be able to learn the picks and adjustments against man and zone coverage. The slant route is the end's most important route. This route keeps the backside off the quarterback. For this position, you should consider any individual that can make the slant-route catch.

Slots

Slots are the two quickest individuals in the offense. They should have strong hands and be able to run inside and cut back. They must be able to hang on to the football.

The slot must be able to beat an outside linebacker deep. This position can break the game wide open at anytime. Because of the motion used in most of the plays, this position must be in great condition. He has to be able to run deep for a pass and then run inside on a lead. The motion allows you to put a game-breaker type individual at slot because he will be in many different positions. Size does not matter as much as speed and the ability to catch the football.

The slot must have the heart to block for his counterparts. He also needs the concentration to deal with any audible and Check-With-Me. If he is an outstanding individual, use him in the 60 Series, or move him to fullback if he is physical enough to handle the pounding.

Fullback

The fullback is the toughest and strongest individual on the field. This is the guy you want to lead your team into war. This player needs to be quick enough to get to the hole and hang on to the football. He must also be able to block defensive ends and blitzing linebackers. This player should be quick, but not at the expense of strength, power, and heart.

If you do not have an individual on your team that fits these characteristics, try using the quicker guards and linebackers. If that doesn't work, look for someone with speed and pass-catching ability, and modify your game strategy.

Quarterback

The quarterback needs to lead by his example, not by his mouth. Pressure cannot affect this individual. He must be smart, aggressive, and patient. He acts as your coach on the field. He must know all the positions and their responsibilities.

He must have the ability to take a snap from the center, and have a strong and accurate arm for at least 40 yards. He should have quick feet, but not at the expense of his throwing ability. He must also be able to take a hit without missing plays. The player who can throw, run the option, and meet the intangible qualities discussed in the previous paragraph—this is your quarterback.

Do your best to find a player with these characteristics. If a quarterback candidate isn't immediately obvious, have the team play touch football in groups of eight and make each player rotate as quarterback. First, look for the most accurate arm. Second, check for arm strength and quick release. Third, watch how the quarterback moves back and into the pocket. Determine if he can make adjustments and throw while moving in the pocket. Don't be shocked if you find your quarterback in one of the lineman.

The quarterback is the most important position in the spread option offense. Find that individual and determine his strengths. He may be better at running the option than he is at passing, or better at passing than running the option. But remember, both schemes help set up the other. Even if your quarterback does not excel in both areas, he will have success because defenses will lean towards stopping one phase and leave the other wide open.

CONCLUSION

Many of the plays discussed in this book will work in different formations and motions. If you decide to use the spread option offense, start with the 90 Series. The 90 Series out of the double slot will keep the defense off balance and prepare your offense for any defense.

Thank you for reading this book. I have worked many years on the fundamentals, techniques, and concepts of the spread option. I don't expect any coach to use the entire offense, so examine what might help your program and remember to use balanced formations, motion, audibles, option, and picks.

GLOSSARY

0 Route:	A fade route.
0-1-2 Rule:	The quarterback counts the number of safety defenders (0, 1, or 2) to determine the play.
1 Route:	A slant route.
2 Route:	A five-yard flat route.
2i:	A defensive tackle playing slightly inside the playside guard. A 2i usually will pinch into the A gap.
3 Route:	A five-yard hook route.
4 Route:	An eight to ten yard out route.
4i:	A defensive tackle aligned on the inside eye of the offensive tackle. Usually the 4i will come on a B-gap slant.
5 Route:	Ten-yard curl.
6 Route:	Fifteen to thirteen-yard comeback.
7 Route:	A post route.
8 Route:	A flag or corner route.
9 Route:	A postcurl route.
50:	The defense has three down linemen versus the slot/twins, or five down linemen versus the flanker/wing.
Audible:	The quarterback changes the play on the line of scrimmage.
B:	A receiver is called to block on a pass or hitch.
Box:	The area of the offensive line.
Check-With-Me:	The quarterback calls a play in the huddle, but calls the hole direction on the line of scrimmage.
Chop Block:	The offensive linemen cut their defenders in the thighs.
Combo Block:	Two offensive linemen double-team block a defensive lineman up to a linebacker.
D Route:	A drag route where a receiver runs across the field climbing to 15 yards.
F Route:	A flare route.
Fan:	A seven step dropback pass on which the offensive linemen take two heel-toe back steps as they are blocking big on big.
Hot Receiver:	A receiver running slant, fade, bubble, dump, hitch, flat, or hook. He should be looking for the ball by the third step.

Jab Block:	The offensive line pass blocks aggressively by popping their hands directly into the defenders' chests.
L Route:	The receiver quickly looks for the pass on the inside seam.
Larry:	Long motion by the right back. The back will align between the two strongside receivers.
Lassie:	Extra-long lateral motion by the right back. The back will cross all receivers to the opposite side of the formation.
Lateral Motion:	Medium, long, and extra-long motion. It is not short motion.
Levels:	A combination of predetermined routes. The outside receiver runs a flag. The second playside receiver runs an out and the third playside receiver runs a flat. All backside receivers run drags and posts. Levels is used mainly in bootlegs.
Lip:	Medium motion by the right back. The back will come lateral and stop near the front side open tackle or tight end.
Lou:	Short motion by the right back to the left into the I formation.
Me:	A line call made by the playside guard. It is directed at the playside tackle in a trap play. *Me* tells the playside tackle to base block because the playside guard will release inside and block the playside middle backer.
Mirror Routes:	The outside receivers on both sides run the same route and the inside receivers on both sides run the same route.
Nut Block:	The offensive line fires out hard and low at the defenders' thighs on a Quick Pass attempt. This will help keep the defenders' hands down.
On the Go:	Teaching fundamentals and techniques without interrupting the flow of practice.
Pick Route:	A receiver runs his given route, but shields the defender who is covering the near receiver running the under route. Also called a rub.
Pitchman:	The back that is going to get the pitch from the quarterback in the option.
Position Read:	The quarterback reads a specific secondary defender and throws in the opposite direction of his drop.
Presnap Read:	The quarterback determines his primary receiver on the line of scrimmage, before the ball is snapped.
Progression Read:	The quarterback determines before the snap what specific receivers to read because they will come open according to a progression.

Quick:	A three-step dropback pass that tells the offensive line to aggressively pass block on the line of scrimmage.
Reggie:	Long motion by the left back. The back will align between the two strongside receivers.
Rip:	Medium motion by the left back. The back will come lateral and stop near the front-side open tackle or tight end.
Rotate:	The safety comes down to cover a defender or area versus motion.
Rover:	Extra-long lateral motion by the left back. The back will cross all receivers to the opposite side of the formation.
Roy:	Short motion by the left back. This back aligns in the I formation.
S Route:	An out and up.
Rub:	A receiver runs a pick for another receiver. Also called a pick route.
Scripting:	A list of written plays for the team segment of practice or the first few plays of a game.
Set Step:	An offensive lineman takes one very quick heel-toe hinge back step in order to invite a defensive lineman to run upfield. This step tries to show pass by extending the arms forward.
Strong:	The side of the offensive alignment towards motion.
Stop:	A five-step dropback pass in which the offensive line takes one heel-toe back step as they are blocking big on big.
Trips Combinations:	A motion man comes across the formation and is on the same side as the other two receivers. The outside receiver runs the first-route number, the second receiver runs the second-route number, and the motion man runs the third-route number.
Under Block:	The playside tight end comes underneath the playside tackle's out block and blocks the playside linebacker.
Unwelcome Stranger:	A backside defender (secondary or linebacker) who runs across the formation with an offensive back in motion.
Weak:	The side of the offensive alignment away from motion.
You:	A call made by the playside guard on a trap play. *You* tells the playside tackle to block the playside linebacker.

Bobby Granger has been a public school teacher and coach for 19 years. He has coached at nine different Texas high schools, including stints as offensive coordinator at Kerriville Ingram High School and San Antonio's John F. Kennedy High School and as quarterback coach at Corpus Christi Miller High School.

Granger began his coaching career at New Braunfels Smithson Valley in Texas, where he was the head baseball coach and freshman football coach. In addition to his work on the high school level, Granger coached receivers for the San Antonio Force arena football team under Head Coach Dick Nolan in 1991.

A native of San Antonio, Texas, Granger graduated from Converse Judson High School. He earned a Bachelor's in Education from Southwest Texas State University in 1983.